TWAYNE'S WORLD AUTHORS SERIES (TWAS)

A Survey of the World's Literature

Sylvia E. Bowman, Indiana University

GENERAL EDITOR

FRANCE

Maxwell A. Smith, Guerry Professor of French, Emeritus
The University of Chattanooga
Visiting Professor in Modern Languages
The Florida State University

EDITOR

François Villon

(TWAS 50)

TWAYNE'S WORLD AUTHORS SERIES (TWAS)

The purpose of TWAS is to survey the major writers
—novelists, dramatists, historians, poets, philosophers,
and critics—of the nations of the world. Among the
national literatures covered are those of Australia,
Canada, China, Eastern Europe, France, Germany,
Greece, India, Italy, Japan, Latin America, New Zea-
land, Poland, Russia, Scandinavia, Spain, and the
African nations, as well as Hebrew, Yiddish, and
Latin Classical literatures. This survey is comple-
mented by Twayne's United States Authors Series
and English Authors Series.

The intent of each volume in these series is to present
a critical-analytical study of the works of the writer;
to include biographical and historical material that
may be necessary for understanding, appreciation,
and critical appraisal of the writer; and to present all
material in clear, concise English—but not to vitiate
the scholarly content of the work by doing so.

François Villon

by Robert Anacker

Twayne Publishers, Inc. :: New York

MANUFACTURED IN THE UNITED STATES OF AMERICA

Preface

This monograph on François Villon is not conceived as a
work of scholarship. It is merely a presentation of the great
poet to readers not familiar with fifteenth-century French. It
is therefore almost entirely based on the text itself, a text
which has been authoritatively established by nineteenth-
century scholars. This text is here described and commented
on in the light of available knowledge of Villon's circumstances. The parts of his work which seemed, quite sub-
jectively, to be the most significant have been paraphrased
in English with utmost care for overtones and other in-
tangibles. Inasmuch as this required an absolutely sure
knowledge of the language, it may be said to stand on a
sound scholarly base, but in the main it rests on an intuitive
penetration of the poet's personality.

As for our knowledge of Villon's life, all the work which
provided us with a few unchallengeable data was likewise
completed in the last century. Very little has since been
added. The archives have been so thoroughly searched that
no document containing a reference to Villon could have
escaped detection. Nor is it likely that new source material
might accidentally be found in European libraries. All au-
thentic information on Villon's life is based on what we
would now call his "police record," namely letters of pardon,
depositions of witnesses, records of court procedure, documents which are at best kept in archives, but certainly not
copied or printed to be put into private or public libraries.
The same scholar who established the authoritative text,
Auguste Longnon, has also compiled all the information

gained from such sources. To this could later be added some information on the persons mentioned by Villon. This research finally led to Champion's work on Villon's life and time, which was first published in Paris in 1913.

In order to paint a picture of Villon, the man and the poet, from the text of his works, the additional information needed to be supplied only in fully integrated form. A detailed itemization in the shape of reference notes seemed entirely superfluous.

I wish to express my sincere thanks to Dr. Maxwell A. Smith, the editor of the French Series, for many valuable hints and corrections. I also thank the publishers of Bantam Books, Inc., for their kind permission to use Anthony Bonner's excellent translation of some passages I did not choose to paraphrase in my own words.

ROBERT ANACKER
Chattanooga, Tennessee

Contents

Chronology

1415   Henry V resumes the war with France. Battle of Agincourt: the English infantry decisively defeats the French knights. The duchy of Burgundy (Burgundy proper plus present-day northern France, Belgium, Luxemburg, and the Netherlands) forms alliance with England.

1420   Treaty of Troyes. Henry V marries Katherine, the daughter of the King of France, and is declared heir to the kingdom. All territory north of the Loire is ceded to England.

1422   Infant king Henry VI is recognized as King of France and England. His regent in France is the able Duke of Bedford. Charles VII, declared illegitimate by his own mother, holds on to his title and is recognized south of the Loire.

1428–   The English lay siege to Orléans, the last stronghold
1429   on the Loire. Joan of Arc is told by her "voices" to "kick the English out of France." She convinces Charles VII of her mission and is given permission to rescue Orléans with 2,000 rough and undisciplined soldiers. She forces the English to withdraw. Then she leads Charles VII to Reims, in the middle of enemy country, where he can be properly crowned. This makes him the legitimate king, regardless of his mother's allegations. In September, Joan attempts in vain to take Paris.

1430   Joan is captured at Compiègne and sold to the English.

1431   After a trial that was a flagrant mockery of justice, Joan is convicted of heresy and witchcraft and burned alive. In the same year Villon is born.

1436   The English leave Paris.

1440–   The French armies, equipped with the excellent artil-
1455   lery purchased by Jacques Coeur, gradually drive the English out of France, leaving only Calais in their hands.

1449   Montcorbier (Villon?) becomes Bachelor of Arts.

1452   Montcorbier graduates as Master of Arts.

1455   Feast of Corpus Christi. Villon's fight with Chermoie (Sermoise), who dies of his wound. First flight from Paris. Letters of remission.

1456   Christmas time. Burglary at the College of Navarre. Villon writes his "Legacy" before leaving Paris.

1461   Villon is freed from the dungeon of Meung by the fortuitous passage of the new king, Louis XI, through the town.

1461   Villon begins writing his "Testament."

1462   Villon is imprisoned in the Châtelet and soon released, but his part in the great burglary has been discovered, and he must pay back his share of the theft.

1462   Villon is imprisoned again and sentenced to be hanged. He appeals to the Parlement.

1463   Death sentence is annulled, and Villon is exiled from Paris. He must have died soon after. Where, when, and how are unknown.

CHAPTER 1

The Images

WRITING about François Villon does not mean intro-
ducing a total stranger. In fact, at the mention of his
name some sort of image is conjured up in many people's
minds. The peculiar thing, however, is that the images so
conjured up differ widely from one another, depending on
the information received or on the manner in which the
information was transmitted.

These images are so different as to be, in many cases,
mutually exclusive. The "nature poet" who "sang as the birds
sing" is hardly compatible with the great patriot who served
as an undercover agent; the gay tavern minstrel does not
easily fit into the role of the hardened criminal who could
laugh at the gallows to which he had been sentenced for
just cause; the ever disappointed, but never disillusioned
Romantic lover cannot be brought in line with the cynical
brothel-keeper. A widespread image is that of the carefree
vagabond proudly refusing bourgeois comfort and security
for the sake of nomadic freedom; another is that of the un-
realistic dreamer who quite unknowingly became involved
with a gang of thieves and thus was forced out of the quiet
scholarly life he cherished.

Such images continue to be elaborated, and new ones are
still being formed. Beatniks and hippies of the 1960s hailed
Villon as a brother, as did the bohemians of a century ago.
He has also been hailed as a brother by such different poets
as Swinburne and Ezra Pound.[1] Among those who hailed
him as a brother we find even the classical French critic,
the "Legislator of Mount Parnassus," Nicolas Boileau.

This large number of divergent images causes one to wonder. How was it possible that Swinburne, a Victorian engaged in mild, purely verbal rebellion against Victorianism, could feel akin to Villon? Where in Villon's works could one find the "beloved vagabond," or the great patriot, or the languishing Romantic lover? What could Boileau have had in mind when he saw in Villon a worthy forerunner?

Of all the posthumous honors bestowed on Villon, this last one is indeed the strangest, but it is also the easiest to dismiss, even before a scrutiny of Villon's works has been made. Quite evidently, Boileau never read a line of Villon. But he had a friend, Patru, whose judgment he valued, and Patru had read at least some of Villon's poems and had found them good. Patru, as would be expected, was much more impressed with Villon's mastery of the external form than with the strikingly personal contents. He had told Boileau that Villon was a remarkable poet, and, to Boileau, that estimate was enough. He did not check. In his opinion the twelve centuries that had passed between the "Fall of Rome" and the advent of Louis XIV were one long period of crudeness and barbarism. Again he did not check. He also knew vaguely that at some time within that age romances had been told in clumsy verse. Villon, he concluded, must have been a writer of romances, and Patru's praise could only mean that he had applied Boileau's rules of good taste to his romances. Hence the two lines:

Villon sut le premier, dans ces siècles grossiers,
Débrouiller l'art confus de nos vieux romanciers.[2]

(Villon was the first in those crude centuries to know how to disentangle the confused art of our old romancers.)

Nothing could have been less to the point. But, after all, very few men like to investigate the foundations of their own prejudices. Boileau was no exception.

Thus the image of Villon as a forerunner of Boileau has

been dismissed. A scrutiny of Villon's work and of the scanty information we have about his life will quickly cause some of the other accepted images to vanish in thin air, whereas others will be found linked to provable reality by at least one thread, or perhaps even two.

The purpose of this study is to make such a scrutiny. It is necessary, therefore, to begin by establishing Villon's place in time and sketching in broad lines the world to which he belonged.

Any vision of times past is necessarily a composite picture obtained from the most different sources, not all of them "historical" or even verbal. A Flemish miniature can be a much more reliable source than a book of unchallenge-able scholarship; contemporary writers of fiction may furnish better insights into the mood of their age than the most conscientiously critical chronicler. The following is a digest of impressions obtained in more than half a lifetime from literally hundreds of sources. To burden this sketch with notes and references would be entirely out of place.

CHAPTER 2

The World He Lived In

AT THE beginning of his "Testament," Villon himself gives the year of his birth. He writes that he was thirty years old when the new king, Louis XI, came through Meung, the occasion also of Villon's release from prison. This was in 1461. Consequently, our poet was born in 1431, the year in which Joan of Arc, or, in Villon's words, "Jeanne, the good girl from Lorraine," was burned alive in Rouen.

He also states very clearly that he was born in Paris. In his famous *Quatrain*, the ironical epitaph of a man about to be hanged, Villon says:

> Je suis Françoys, dont il me poise,
> Né de Paris emprès Pontoise,
> Et de la corde d'une toise
> Sçaura mon col que mon cul poise.

> (I am François, sorry to say,
> born in Paris, near Pontoise,
> and at the end of a rope one *toise* long
> my neck will know the weight of my arse.)

Now there actually have been some scholars who missed the point in the line "born in Paris, near Pontoise," and suggested emendations, putting in place of "Paris" the name of some neighboring village even smaller than Pontoise. They simply could not see the joke. "Paris, near Pontoise" is like saying "New York, near Yonkers." After all, the Paris which is near Pontoise is a very special place.

Yet Villon's Paris was still far from being the great world

center it was to become centuries later. At the time of Villon's birth it was still occupied by the English; even after their expulsion the kings of France much preferred to reside elsewhere. The Loire, not the Seine, was the main artery of France. When the poets sang of Sweet France they had Touraine in mind. Nor did Paris lead in worldly elegance. The centers of refined living were all in the domains of the dukes of Burgundy; no place in the kingdom could compare in splendor with Ghent, Brussels, Antwerp, or even Dijon. From Ghent came the new fashions; at the Burgundian court was staged the last revival of chivalry with all its lavish extravagance; at the same time, in the Burgundian Netherlands the new class of the money-wealthy bourgeoisie first rose to recognized preponderance.

Compared to Brussels, Paris was a poor city. It had one institution, however, that Brussels did not have and of which it was inordinately proud: a university.

I *The University*

This famous school, to be sure, was no longer quite as great as it had been in the days of Abelard and Peter Lombard, but it still had recently produced such clearthinking logicians as Gerson and Pierre d'Ailly, and the other eminent men who represented France so well at the Councils of Constance and Basel.

At the University of Paris, as elsewhere, the student began with the study of the seven liberal arts. The courses were lectures in the true sense of the word, as the teacher usually read aloud to the students from one or the other of the few books that were available. The first "degree" was the Baccalaureate, after which the student could take a more active part in debates and discussions. Thus he prepared himself for his "license" to teach and, soon after, for the degree of Master of Arts. This degree entitled him to pursue higher, more specialized studies at the "faculties." At Paris, in Villon's days, there were the faculties of theology, philosophy, and canon law, but none of jurisprudence or civil law, and none of medicine.

The word "university" had originally been used, and continued to be used, to designate any organized group of men with a community of purpose, such as an artisans' guild. Even in its specific reference to the academic world it meant the closed, regulated corporation of teachers and students rather than the school itself. Founded and fostered by the Church, this corporation was regarded as a branch of the Church. Its members were clerics, even if they had no intention ever to take holy orders. As clerics they were normally exempt from civil jurisdiction; they could be judged only by ecclesiastical courts.

Modern readers are sometimes taken aback by the large number of unsavory characters found in the ranks of the medieval clergy. We are accustomed to see in a priest or a minister a man following a call and therefore sincerely dedicated to his work; if he is not sincere, we quickly condemn him as a hypocrite. It is well to remember that such standards could not possibly apply to the age preceding Reformation and Counter-Reformation, since only very few men became clergymen by choice. Where there was choice, the motives did not have to be a special call or a strong desire to administer spiritual help. A priest had an easier life than a farmer or a soldier; he did not have to worry as much as a merchant. Such lures attracted the weak and the lazy, and if a person was already criminally inclined, the ecclesiastical state offered protection from the extremely harsh civil justice.

II *Renaissance or Middle Ages*

To ask whether the age of Villon belongs to the Middle Ages or to the Renaissance would amount to a mere juggling with words that have no clear meaning, but a host of connotations. To most people the term "fifteenth century" immediately suggests Middle Ages; but if you speak to an Italian about the "Quatrocento," which means the same thing, he will understand you to be referring to an already advanced stage of the Renaissance. This discrepancy in the use of historical terms is usually glossed over by the statement that Italy was so much more "advanced" than the rest of Europe—at any rate fundamentally different. This notion can hardly be maintained in view of the intense relations, commercial and cultural, between Italy and the North. To mention only one point: from the Flemish masters the Italian painters learned the techniques of oil painting and the importance of perspective. Periodization in history is always arbitrary. It is undeniable that many medieval features and attitudes survived in the fifteenth century—some of them survive today—but they survived in Italy to the same degree as elsewhere. Yet it may well be said that by 1400 the chief characteristics of the medieval period had vanished.

So, for instance, money had come back into general use. If there had been money in circulation in the tenth century, there would never have been a feudal system. In warfare, infantry had long since become the decisive arm, rendering armored knights obsolete. It is sometimes stated that firearms made the difference, but firearms came long after the change. Armored knights were slaughtered at Crécy by the English longbowmen, at Nicopolis by the swordfighting Janissaries, and many times by the Swiss pikemen long before portable firearms came into use. Infantry tactics had been developed in all European countries. The Florentines had been glad to hire one John Hawkwood to lead their army.

Along with the return of money and the coming up of infantry, the period had witnessed a gigantic development of the spirit of enterprise. Again, if this can be seen most clearly in Italy, it was by no means limited to that country.

A man like Jacques Coeur of Bourges[3] had outsmarted the most astute Italian businessmen. In Germany, too, the cloth merchants of Augsburg were beginning to build up their princely fortunes by engaging in a variety of enterprises not connected with their original trade. That new spirit of enterprise was alive on both sides of the Alps; in fact, there was very little difference. Italians who had to travel or even chose to live in the North would complain about the climate, but would certainly not feel too keen a difference in the way of life.

So the question whether Villon belongs to the Renaissance or to the Middle Ages is entirely irrelevant. Inasmuch as he externally followed the conventions of medieval poetry—only to be all the more unconventional in essence—one might recognize in his work many a trait that reminds of the Troubadours. On the other hand, one of the most characteristic phenomena of the Renaissance is the powerful self-assertion of the artist, and in that respect Villon is indeed a man of that age.

III   *Aftermath of the War and Natural Calamities*

By the time Villon reached his manhood, the war, which was said to have lasted a hundred years, had at last simply discontinued without a peace treaty or even an armistice. The French, after losing most of the battles, had unquestionably won the war; the English, who still held Paris at the time of Villon's birth, were now driven out of every French town except Calais. There was no danger of their renewing the war, for the incredibly savage Wars of the Roses were using up the last remnants of their once formidable military strength.

France was victorious, but in an indescribable state of exhaustion and devastation, and she continued to be ravaged long after the cessation of hostilities. The soldiers who were no longer needed could not be paid. They had no means of subsistence other than banditry; they terrorized the country-side and kept all food from the cities. It took great and consistent efforts on the part of the royal government gradually to build up the finances again until some of these bandits could be formed into a regular standing army of sufficient strength to annihilate the rest of them.

These calamities affected all of France, but during the years of Villon's childhood Paris had to suffer a long series of unusual hardships. When the English left in 1436, they took everything with them. Hundreds of Frenchmen died of hunger because food could only be obtained on the black market at fantastic prices. In addition to such hardships as were the direct consequence of the war, there occurred a number of unusual natural catastrophes. Paris, which normally has mild winters, experienced one of uncommon severity in 1439 when it snowed continually for forty days. Because fuel was as short as food, other hundreds froze to death. Famished wolves found ways of entering the city and they not only dug out corpses, but also killed several children and two women before they could be exterminated. The summer before, an epidemic, probably smallpox, had taken many lives. The last of these natural calamities was the most unusual: a windstorm of great violence brought down chimneys, church steeples, and a number of houses.

But France is a naturally rich country. As soon as some order was restored, food became available, business picked up, and normal life could be resumed.

IV *Recovery and* Joie de Vivre

Life was still rather wild by any standards. After the incredible privations, the things of this world had to be enjoyed to the full. Morals were what they usually are except in times of puritanical repression. Hundreds of prostitutes were available, and every fashionable inn or lodging house had to be well provided with them. A contemporary French miniature shows travelers arriving at an inn; beds are ready, and in every bed a woman is waiting, decently covered with the sheet up to her neck.

In addition to the regular licensed and organized prostitutes there were many semi-prostitutes. These were young married women who helped the family budget by earning a few pennies and whose husbands often acted as their pimps. To this class most of the women mentioned in Villon's poems must have belonged, notably "La Belle Heaumière" whose name indicates that she must have been the wife of a helmet maker or armorer.

Generally speaking, all these people, including prostitutes, pimps, and thieves, regarded themselves as good Christians. They believed in the teachings of the Church and hoped to attain salvation. They knew they were indulging in sin, quite often in more than one of the capital ones, but they blamed human weakness. The Church kept telling them that God is mericful, that anyone who truly repents his sins will be pardoned. Therefore, they were all determined to repent sooner or later, but there was no need of too great a hurry. To be sure, many sincere men and women, horrified at the surrounding depravity, practiced severe asceticism as the way of atoning for the failures of the weak.

V *The City*

No reliable figures exist as to the population of towns and cities. A fair estimate gives Villon's Paris about forty thousand inhabitants crowded together in a rather limited space. On the right bank the inner ring of the present boulevards indicates the location of the walls; on the left bank the city limits barely included the present Latin Quarter. The abbey of St. Germain des Prés, as its name reveals, was already out in the fields. The streets were narrow, and the overhanging upper stories blocked much of the light and air. Since the innumerable signs of shops and taverns always stood at right angles to the houses, they could be a real obstacle. Good old maître Jean Cotard, who was always drunk and thirsty for more, once had a huge bump on his head from a butcher's sign that wouldn't get out of his way.

VI   *Dress*

Men and women dressed elegantly, extravagantly if they could afford it. Surely the shopkeepers' wives and half prostitutes of Villon's acquaintance dressed fashionably. Perhaps the material of their dresses was not always the most expensive, but the cut at least was elegant. The gowns were long and very tight at the waist where a beltlike outer bodice held things together. Below, it was ample; there was always at least an indication of a train. Above the waist the gown opened in a very wide V; its edge, usually trimmed, barely covered the breasts. However, an undergarment of a different color, frequently embroidered, came up to a straight line at the height of the collarbones. To this undergarment, a sort of stay or pettycoat, the sleeves were attached by means of ribbons; they could easily be changed. The gown had no sleeves but very large, trimmed arm holes that were called devil's windows. Women wore shoes of many different shapes, but no hose. Some of the most affluent wore a long linen shirt underneath the undergarment. That, if it was worn at all, was the only piece of lingerie in a woman's dress.

Unmarried girls wore their hair long and let it hang down freely over back and shoulders. A permissible alternative was to wear it in long tresses. Married women always completely covered their hair; at home, with a cap or a kerchief, in the street and on festive occasions, with a tall hat. The most characteristic feminine headdress was the *hennin,* a conical hat about two feet long from whose apex a light veil hung down over the back. There were also hennins shaped like truncated cones as well as cylindrical ones. The Flemish paintings show some truly fantastic women's hats of the oddest shapes. They were all very high and had the veil in the back; they all hid the hair completely; and over the forehead, where some strands might have protruded, the hair was cleanly shaved off.

With the men, too, the shirt was a luxury item with which many dispensed. All men wore breeches of cloth. They were very short, barely covering the seat and the upper thighs, held in place by a belt. To the breeches were fastened the *houseaux,* or hose, a sort of leggings cut out of cloth. For the tailor this was the most difficult piece to fit properly. There was no knitted or otherwise elastic material, yet the leg had to be molded perfectly. The degree to which this elegant tightening was attained depended largely on the means of the wearer. On the legs of peasants and work-men the paintings show sloppily fitted hose. At the upper end the hose was fastened to the breeches with a large number of thongs. When Joan of Arc first donned men's clothes, she complained about the many laces she had to tie. The hose reached down over the ankle and was held tight by a strap underneath the foot. Only the very wealthy could afford the new kind of hose that enclosed the entire foot and had a leather sole underneath—in other words, a combination of stocking and shoe. Most men wore separate shoes on their bare feet, as did the women.

In the coats of the men the greatest possible variety is found: wide, close-fitting to tight, long or short. Each type of coat had its special name. As a rule, clerics and profes-sional men such as doctors or lawyers wore long coats; merchants and artisans, short ones. Young noblemen are usually shown in very short and incredibly tight coats. As for Villon, since he was a cleric, we may assume that he usually wore a long coat coming down at least to his knees, if not farther.

VII *Hygiene, Food, Drink*

The people so attired kept reasonably clean. At home the weekly bath, in a wooden tub, seems to have been the rule. For travelers, outside visitors, or other persons who had to live in inns, the public bath was available for a moderate fee. To be sure, the public bath offered attractions other than an opportunity to get clean, but bathing was part of it. As a rule, people in Villon's day still had high standards of bodily cleanliness. The period of utter neglect was not to come until a century later.

Their diet was not greatly varied. Barley porridge, oatmeal, and other forms of gruel played an important part. The term "daily bread" was not a figure of speech. Since most of the green vegetables we know today—green beans, sweet peas, not to speak of such typical American products as the tomato, the potato, and corn were totally unknown —lettuce and various kinds of cabbage were about the only source of vitamins other than fresh fruit. The chief supply of protein, in towns not too distant from the sea, came in form of salted herrings. One of the greatest revolutions in the history of human economics had just been brought about by the herring's decision to shift its spawning grounds from the Baltic Sea to the North Sea, a shift which caused the decline of the Hanseatic League and the rapid rise of Amsterdam from a poor fishing village to a world center.

Fresh meat was available in great quantity around St. Martin's Day in November. At that time most of the cattle were slaughtered, since only the best heads could be expected to survive the winter. Hay was made only in small quantity; all arable land was used for the production of grain. While the meat was fresh, people gorged themselves with it. What they could not eat right away was salted and kept in large barrels. Toward spring, when Lent was over, this salted meat required considerable spicing to remain palatable; hence that great demand for pepper which ultimately was to lead to the discovery of America. Smoked hams and sides of bacon were preferred to corned beef. Another, more refined method of meat preservation, sausage making, was already the specialty of certain towns whose names, such as Bologna, Frankfurt, Vienna, Braunschweig, have been immortalized to this day. For the very wealthy, fresh meat was available the year round, and they could also indulge in such delicacies as bird pastry or piglets cooked inside a whole ox. The nobles also had the privilege to provide themselves with venison.

In judging the drinking habits of these people, the modern reader must remember that there was no hard liquor. The art of distilling, although known to the alchemists, had not yet been applied to the mass production and easy availability of strong spirits. But France, then as now, was the land of good wines, and wine in sufficient quantity will have its effects. There are records of the unbelievable amounts of wine consumed at municipal dinners. When kings and dukes feasted one another, or when the knights of the Golden Fleece, the flower of chivalry, banqueted at one of their reunions, it was expected that every participant would have to be carried away drunk. Quite generally, a host was despised as a miser if his guest had not become inebriated. There are letters of thanks in which we can read: " . . . your Gracious Highness has treated me so well that in the course of ten days I have not been sober a single moment. . . ."

It is not necessary here to dwell on the gloomy, pessimistic side of the fifteenth-century mentality. Many historians have seen in those aspects the true face of the age. Yet this incessant preoccupation with death, this fear of being snatched away too suddenly for repentance, this inescapable presence of some *memento mori* at every turn—these traits merely complete the picture of a society bursting with vitality and enjoying with unashamed gusto all the pleasures of the flesh.

CHAPTER 3

What We Know of His Life

I   *His Name*

"JE SUIS Françoys," Villon says in his bravado *Quatrain*, and, in fact, that is the only statement which can be made with absolute certainty concerning his name. François was the name he was given in baptism. As for his last name, it must be remembered that in his days the use of patronymic names was not yet rigidly fixed. A person could freely choose his second name. As a mature man, François chose the name of his benefactor, Guillaume Villon, at whose house he had lived as a student. There is no indication that the man was his uncle, although some of the more imaginative biographers have so asserted. Villon is what François called himself as a poet, the name he often inserted in his poems in form of an acrostic. But there never was a youth by that name registered at the university.

What was his name when he was still a student? On this point the official documents still available are of little help, for they give us two different names for what must be the same man. The two documents in question are both letters of remission, or full pardons, for an act of justifiable manslaughter. Both are dated January, 1455, which would be the year 1456 by our calendar. In one of them, which was issued by the royal chancery court then on circuit in Saint-Pourçain, in the province of Bourbonnais, the recipient of the pardon is named "François des Loges, alias Villon." The other was issued by the permanent chancery court of Paris; in it the man guilty of unquestionably the same manslaughter is named François de Montcorbier, with no alias given.

This is indeed strange. In spite of the fact that the two pardons refer to the same case, some doubt has been raised as to the identity of the pardoned men. Why should Villon have used one name in addressing the royal court and another in appealing to the court in Paris? Furthermore, it is only after the name "des Loges" that the words "autrement dit de Villon" occur. The name "des Loges," on the other hand, is not found in any other official document, whereas Montcorbier is frequently mentioned.

Was our poet the man known to the Parisian authorities as Montcorbier? Much of our conjectural biography hinges on that identity. It was Montcorbier who obtained his baccalaureate in 1449 and his degree of Master of Arts in 1452. The evidence gathered by Longnon was sufficient to convince the great scholar Gaston Paris[4] of this identity. It is therefore possible, though by no means certain, that Montcorbier was Villon's name at the time he became a student. This still would not mean that it was the name of his father.

This father, whom Villon had never consciously known, is referred to as a poor man of humble extraction in Stanza 35 of the "Testament." This line clearly shows that in spite of the highsounding name of de Montcorbier—if this indeed was Villon's name—the ancient nobility which some fanciful biographers have bestowed on him is pure fiction.

Villon's mother, on the other hand, was still alive when he wrote his "Testament." He describes her as a poor old woman who has suffered much anguish and grief on his account, and he dedicates to her one of his most poignantly beautiful poems.

II   *Student Days*

As a student, Villon led a gay life. In Paris, as in Oxford and elsewhere, there was constant friction between gown and town. The students took full advantage of being exempt from the jurisdiction of the civil authorities and engaged in the wildest pranks. Even if we had no proof of it, we could safely guess that Villon was a ringleader in some of the more imaginative exploits. One of those affairs, although quite ludicrous in itself, had repercussions out of all proportion and is therefore well documented.

On the property of a certain Mademoiselle de Bruyères there was a peculiarly shaped stone, probably a prehistoric monument, that was generally known as "Le Pet au Diable" ("The Devil's Fart"). One day the students removed this famous stone from its site and dragged it to their quarter. Thereupon the owner of the house filed a wordy complaint, claiming that the stone was her property. The police then went to retrieve it and placed it, for safekeeping, in the courtyard of the Palace of Justice.

This the students could not tolerate. They contrived to to enter the forbidden premises and brought the stone back to their quarter. For good measure they removed another stone from Mademoiselle de Bruyères' yard, named it "La Vesse" ("The Silent Fart"), and proceded to "marry" the two stones in great ceremony. This mock wedding pleased the students so well that they now began to steal signs from shops and taverns to unite them also in mock matrimony.

This time the authorities became angry. Robert d'Estouteville, the provost, invaded the students' quarter with a large body of men and had the two stones and all the stolen signs removed. As usual, there was a good deal of brutality, and the policemen also took things they should not have taken. This invasion was a serious infringement on the rights of the university. Professors and students united in protest. They went on strike and appealed to higher ecclesiastical authority. It was the usual deadlock. The conflict between the respective authorities lasted for years. The students regarded this as a state of open warfare and harrassed the town authorities as much as they could.

It is highly probable that Villon's first literary effort was a prose novel, *Le Pet au Diable*, in which he told the whole story. It was widely circulated among the students, and it is known that several copies were made. None of these have survived.

III *Villon's Involvement with the Police*

The incident which caused Villon to flee from Paris for the first time happened on June 5, 1455, three years after Montcorbier's graduation as Master of Arts. It was the Feast of Corpus Christi. Villon was sitting outside near the church of Saint Benoît le Bétourné where Guillaume Villon was chaplain. Talking with a girl and a priest, he was suddenly attacked by another priest, Chermoie or Sermoise. At the first exchange of words the witnesses fled. It seems that the priest struck first. He came at Villon with a large dagger and cut his upper lip very badly. François then struck him with a little dagger, wounding him in the groin. At first, Chermoie did not even notice that he was wounded and kept coming at Villon. Another friend, who had not seen the beginning of the fray, interfered. He disarmed Villon to prevent further mischief, but as Chermoie continued to threaten him with his dagger, Villon felled him by throwing a rock at his head. Then he went to a barber-surgeon to have his wound dressed, and there he gave his name as Michel Mouton (Sheep).

All would have been well if Chermoie had not died of his wound in the hospital where he had been taken. Villon had to leave Paris as fast as he could. The following January, having received two valid pardons, he could safely return.

Thus his first known involvement with the law seems to have been a case of self-defense. Quite probably, however, it was not his first criminal act.

Here we may ask: How was it possible that a young man who had had the advantages of an education could become a criminal? It is not very difficult to answer this question.

In the first place, there is no clear dividing line between "swiping things for fun" and actual stealing. Later tradition, kept alive among the Paris students, credits Villon with a remarkable ability to provide excellent suppers for himself and his friends, of course without paying. The master thief is a hero in folklore. All famous pranksters, such as Till Eulenspiegel and Nazreddin Hodja,[5] possess incomparable ingenuity when it comes to robbing merchants and inn-keepers. The "swiping" of a ridiculous stone from some-body's property is an innocent prank; the stealing of a person's money is a crime. The technique is the same.

There is another point. For an educated man there were not very many opportunities in Villon's day. He could have been apprenticed to a notary and thus have earned a pit-tance. Very few clerics had a chance to become the secre-taries of lords and bishops or perhaps stewards on some large estate. Even if he took holy orders, Villon would still be a priest without a prebend, perhaps a starving vicar in some village church. The monasteries and the houses of the mendicant friars were crowded; they had long since stopped accepting anybody who came along. Even to retire from the world, a man needed recommendations such as poor François was not likely to obtain.

Furthermore, we must remember that in Villon's days there was an entirely different attitude in regard to crime. Crime today is seen as an act endangering society. This concept goes back to the great criminologists of the eigh-teenth century. Earlier ages, however, simply saw criminal acts as sin: it is a sin to steal, just as lechery and gluttony are sins; murder is bad because the Ten Commandments forbid killing. Gaston Paris, in his discussion of this point, quotes the chronicle in which the deeds of the discharged soldiers are described. After telling how they robbed travel-ers, how they tortured peasants to make them reveal where the money was hidden, how they waylaid honest women and even immature girls to use them for their lust, the chronicler adds that they also ate meat during Lent. To his mind, this sin was as bad as the others.

What crimes did Villon commit? On the basis of our scanty information we can charge him only with theft. He seems also to have been well familiar with loaded dice and other crooked gambling devices. He seems to have been an experienced confidence man. It is not likely that he committed many acts of violence, except that he sometimes became involved in brawls and street fights. But he was a member of a widespread criminal association known as "La Coquille." This organization had its reliable fences in every town and operated brothels where a man could remain safely hidden from justice. They used a secret language, a jargon in which Villon later wrote several poems that defy all attempts at translation.

Shortly before Christmas, 1456, Villon led two expert safe-crackers and a few other bold men to the coffers of the College of Navarre near where he lived. They forced two locks and stole some five hundred écus, a very considerable sum. After that, Villon found it prudent to leave Paris.

IV Relations with Duke Charles d'Orléans

Since legal documents are our only source of information for Villon's biography, we lose all track of him during the time he was hidden from justice. At some time within this period he must have been living in Blois at the court of the Duke of Orléans. This prince of the royal blood, who had spent the greater part of his life as a war prisoner in England, was himself a poet. If anyone could be called the last medieval poet, it would undoubtedly be he. With delicate sensibility he had used all the traditional themes of lyrical poetry, from the pangs of unrequited love to the charms of spring and the rigors of winter. Each of his poems is a gem of light, elegant expression; each is full of carefully restrained feeling. Retired from worldly affairs, he now lived at his castle in Blois, a patron of the arts and especially a protector of fellow poets. He liked to surround himself with them and would often play the fashionable game of holding a poetry contest. He would then give them the theme in the first line and the refrain and let them fill in the rest. If he liked a poem thus composed, he would enter it into his own album of poetry, indicating the name of the author. It is rather astonishing to find a "Ballade Villon" inserted among Duke Charles's pretty poems. The theme was "I am dying of thirst near the fountain," and the refrain "Well received, pushed away by everyone." The idea was that every line should contain an irreconcilable contradiction, and yet the poem as a whole should make some sense. Villon acquitted himself well enough for the duke to preserve his poem. It is, needless to say, not one of his best. Only the last line of the *Envoi,* immediately preceding the refrain, deviates from the given theme in a way characteristic of Villon: "Que fais-je plus? Quoy? Les gaiges ravoir!" ("What more do I do? What? To have my wages again!")

The last words "Les gaiges ravoir" also could mean "to get back things I have pawned." Both interpretations are possible. It could mean that Villon had been on the duke's payroll and that his wages had been withheld, or simply that he wished to redeem things pawned. In either case it amounts to a request for money that brutally contrasts with the sentiments expressed down to this line.

Charles d'Orléans died in 1465. It is therefore possible that Villon's stay at his court, which in any case can only have been short, occurred after his last banishment from Paris. It is more probable that the friendly encounter between the two poets took place some time during his first exile from Paris following the burglary of December, 1456.

A second, very different, involvement with the kindly duke is harder to explain. Among the poems not inserted in the "Testament" is an "Epistle to Marie d'Orléans" in which

Villon states that the birth of this little princess has saved him from death. Here the date is known to be 1457. Everything else remains obscure. Was he really saved from death, or is this just a figure of speech? Why this bombastic praise of an infant girl and her illustrious parents? It could be, of course, that he was released from prison and possible execution on account of the happy event. It was common practice to set prisoners free on days of joy. There is no other clue than the poem itself, and that is nothing but hyperbolical praise.

V   *Imprisonment and Pardon*

We find Villon again in the summer of 1461, this time in chains in a dark dungeon, eating moldy bread and drinking stale water. He had been imprisoned in the castle of Meung by Thibaut d'Aussigny, Bishop of Orléans, no doubt for good cause. He was treated, however, with excessive cruelty and for a time he believed himself abandoned and forgotten by all his friends. It is altogether possible that he would have died in that dungeon if it had not been for the extremely lucky coincidence that the new king, Louis XI, chose that time to ride through Meung on the way to Touraine. Custom was to release all prisoners when a newly anointed king entered a town. This was on October 2, 1461.

Villon was thirty years old at the time, but he probably looked twice that age. Those terrible months in Meung had broken him. Now in Paris, he wrote his "Testament" into which he inserted the most beautiful of his *ballades*.

But his biography depends on legal records, and so we find him again, in prison of course, this time in the Châtelet. The charge cannot have been very serious, for he was about to be released when the officials, going over old records, were reminded of his participation in the burglary at the College of Navarre. That old escapade had come to light in the most unusual manner. One of the lesser participants, a certain Guy Tabarie, had revealed the whole story in an almost incredible bragging spree. Trying to impress some-body, who later turned out to be very much the wrong man, he had alluded to his connections with experienced pick-locks. He himself, he declared, was one of the boys who had "pulled that job" at the College of Navarre, and that certainly had been no small thing. He had no sooner said this than he was denounced to the police. Interrogated with the help of the rack, Tabarie confessed and gave all the names. Of the men he had mentioned, only Villon was now available.

The authorities were fair with him. Since four men had stolen five hundred *écus,* they computed Villon's share at one hundred and twenty *écus.* For this sum he had to sign bond and promise to pay within three years.

Villon had been out of prison less than a month when he was arrested again, this time definitely without sufficient reason. He had been with a group of friends when these started a fight with a lawyer and his clerks. Villon had not taken part in the brawl. He had run away as soon as it began. Nevertheless he had been recognized and was taken to jail.

The former provost, Robert d'Estouteville, had always been as friendly as possible to Villon. In the early days of the students' pranks he had often actually protected him. Villon had paid eloquent homage to him and his wife, Ambroise de Loré, in an early *ballade.* Unfortunately, this understanding man was no longer provost, and his successor seems to have made it a point to be as severe as possible with his predecessor's protégés. Villon was given the terrible water torture and sentenced to be hanged.

It was then that he wrote his bravado *Quatrain* and also his famous *Ballade of the Hanged.* Death at the gallows loomed as a very real possibility. Yet, however bravely he faced death, he decided to appeal to the Parlement of Paris.

This highest court of justice acted favorably. Considering the fact that nobody had been killed in the street fight in question and that all the witnesses said that Villon had fled, it annulled the provost's sentence, but exiled Villon from Paris.

Nothing further is known of Villon's life. The assumption that he withdrew to some quiet corner and continued to live without ever writing another poem is hardly compatible with what we know about his personality. It is generally believed that he died soon after the Parlement had exiled him.

How did he die? Did he return illegally to his beloved Paris and was he hanged? Did the *Coquille* think he had "squealed"? Criminal organizations throughout the centuries have been very consistent in their way of dealing with "squealers." He could also have died of his broken health. One guess is as good as the other.

Preliminary Remarks

THE text used is that of Longnon,[6] which Gaston Paris accepted as authoritative, with the slight corrections of Foulet.

Of the available translations, only one is acceptable, that of Anthony Bonner. It is, of course, altogether impossible to "translate" poetry, especially if one attempts to do it in verse, as have Heron Lepper, John Payne, and, at least for part of Villon's work, Swinburne. Some translations of this type may have the merit of being in themselves literary works of distinction, but much of the original meaning, not to speak of overtones and other intangible qualities is irretrievably lost.

A Chinese scholar of long ago, whose name I can neither remember nor find again, said that the best of translations is to the original what the underside is to a piece of embroidery: all the threads are there. Anthony Bonner's translation of Villon's works has the great advantage of not attempting to render the poetic form; Bonner stresses choice of vocabulary with utmost care for meaning and tone and he resists squeamishness in his design for fidelity to Villon's language.

In most cases I have chosen merely to paraphrase the poems in my own words. Where I preferred to use Bonner's translation, I have indicated this by the sign (B) at the end of the poem.

In order to give the reader an impression of the poetic form, I have in some cases added the French text.

Bonner's translation, incidentally, has recently been published together with Longnon's French text in a paperback Bantam book.

CHAPTER 4

Villon's "Legacy"

AS has been stated, Villon's first work was the prose novel *Le Pet au Diable*, in which he related in full detail the ludicrous affair of the famous stone. Guy Tabarie, the man who later revealed the facts about the burglary at the College of Navarre, is known to have made a copy of this novel. All copies, however, had disappeared by the time Villon's works were set in print.

The first extant work, therefore, is "Les Lais," which is best translated as "Legacy." It consists of forty stanzas of eight lines each, in verses of eight syllables. It is a mock will by which the poet bequeathes a number of worthless things to friends and enemies.

There is nothing original in the idea of a mock will. Humorous wills had been made many times before. Nor is the genre limited to some past age. Every graduating class of a school that still adheres to tradition will have a "class night" in which a class will is read. Even in the rare cases when such a class will is truly witty, it can amuse only those who know the persons mentioned.

The same is true, to a large extent, of Villon's "Lais." Although the scholars have succeeded in identifying many of the persons and telling us a little more about them than we could find in Villon's lines, they remain strangers. The irony, the wit, the humor have evaporated. What remains is an enumeration of names and of ridiculous gifts.

Since it purports to be a legal document, the "Legacy" begins with the date, 1456, and a statement that the writer is sound in mind and a free man. He will take the advice, he says, of the wise old Roman, Vegetius, and put his affairs in order.

Villon's scholarship is always a little questionable. Vegetius was a writer on military tactics late in the fourth century. In his introduction he stresses the importance of order and discipline. It would seem that Villon had not read any further than that, since he praises him only as a wise old counselor.

It is shortly before Christmas, he then states, the dead season when even the wolves have to live on thin air. The reason he has thought of making a will is that he has decided to leave Paris.

Here we pause. Christmas time, 1456, was the time of the daring burglary at the College of Navarre. So we know the real reason for his departure and can enjoy all the more what he has to say about it.

He wishes to escape, Villon says, from the prison of love. She whose charms have held him captive so long has been most cruel. She has not only rejected, but wantonly betrayed him; yes, she has stabbed him to the quick. He must put an end to his suffering by going away from her. Yes, he will go to Angers. It is very hard to leave her, but it must be. If this situation lasted longer, it would be his death. So he will go, a martyr of love. It will be a long journey, and human life is fraught with dangers. In view of this uncertainty, he must make a will before leaving.

It goes without saying that all this is pure fiction—his ladylove, her cruelty and infidelity no less than his martyrdom. Furthermore, it is all as conventional as can be, for these identical sentiments and thoughts have been expressed thousands of times all over Europe, first by the gentlemen poets of the age of chivalry and then by their middle-class successors. Nobody had ever taken such expressions to be fully sincere. It was a fashionable game that had to be played according to the rules; the only freedom for the

player was in rearranging the words. The words themselves
were always the same, as were the themes.

Here the theme chosen is the cruelty of the lady. In
the last analysis, her cruelty consisted merely in refusing
sexual intercourse to her knight. Of course, that was not
what they called it; they called it "the reward," and a man
who had unflinchingly served his lady was entitled to this
reward. The lady could make her cruelty worse by granting
to another what she had denied her servant, and this is what
Villon claims was done to him. Since the beginning of the
twelfth century the theme had been standard.

Some of the earlier scholars who had been brought up in
the Romantic age tried very hard to identify Villon's cruel
ladylove. They had a great choice of names, but none of the
persons finally identified seemed to fit. Gradually, in the
course of looking up documents, they came upon the real
reasons for Villon's departure at precisely that time, namely
the successful robbery at the College of Navarre. Guy
Tabarie, the informer who betrayed Villon and his other
accomplices, said, among other things, that Villon had gone
to Angers in order to perpetrate another crime. In a monas-
tery in Angers, where Villon had an uncle, there also lived
a very old monk who was said to have buried a considerable
sum before retiring from the world. According to Tabarie,
it was Villon's intention to approach this old man through
his uncle and to find out where that money was.

When Robert Louis Stevenson read these revelations as to
Villon's situation in December, 1456, he was truly shocked.
Always torn between his great love of adventure and what
was left of his Scotch upbringing, Stevenson had felt greatly
attracted toward Villon, but certain things were just too
much for him. That Villon should have used the love theme
as a motive for his flight and even mentioned Angers as his
destination—Angers, where he intended to rob an old man—
that was impardonable. It caused Stevenson to reevaluate

Villon, and so he wrote that essay which Gaston Paris said presented too dark a picture ("trop en noir"). In this essay he almost revels in the fact that Villon was an ordinary criminal. He tries to contrast Villon, the great poet, with Villon, the utterly contemptible man, but much as he tries to reject the man it is obvious that he likes him just the same.

So the only true point in the opening stanzas of the "Legacy" is the line: "Adieu, je m'en vois a Angiers" (Good-bye, I'm off to Angers"). All the rest is conventional fiction.

The first bequest goes to his benefactor.

> Premierement, ou nom du Pere,
> Du Filz et du Saint Esperit,
> Et de sa glorieuse Mere
> Par qui grace riens ne perit,
> Je laisse, de par Dieu, mon bruit
> A maistre Guillaume Villon,
> Qui en l'onneur de son nom bruit,
> Mes tentes et mon pavillon.
>
> (First, in the name of the Father,
> the Son and the Holy Spirit,
> and His glorious Mother
> by whose grace none perish,
> I leave, God willing, my reputation
> to master Guillaume Villon
> who shines in the honor of his name,
> my tents and my pavilion.)

This stanza, with the exception of the last, purely ironical line—poor Villon had no tents or pavilion to give away—is strangely prophetic. In 1456 he could not know that in assuming the good old man's name he had made that name immortal. He had taken and given. Who would know anything about Guillaume Villon, a modest chaplain at one of the altars of Saint Benoît le Bétourné, if François had not used his name to give it back to him as a name of lasting fame.

The second gift goes to his fictitious lady. He leaves her his heart, of course, his pale pitiful heart, in a little shrine. This, too, had been said many thousands of times and had even been put into gruesome practice by dying knights who ordered their hearts cut out and sent to their fair ladies.

After this come the humorous gifts to friends, to officials and jailers, and to enemies. The most concrete of those bequests are things that first would have to be redeemed from the pawnshop for a sum of money greater than their worth. He is also generous with shop signs: an official who must do a great deal of riding is given the White Horse, and to a wealthy spice merchant is bequeathed the Golden Mortar. This goes on from stanza XI to stanza XXXIV. Then, in stanza XXXV, the tone changes. Villon hears the bell of the Sorbonne which at nine o'clock announces the curfew and calls for the last Angelus. So he interrupts his work on the will to pray, but in the midst of this he falls asleep. The process of going to sleep, however, is described in the most complicated scholastic jargon. He tells us how Dame Memory picked up and put on shelves the "collateral species," then the "opinative" ones, both false and true, finally the "estimative, prospective, similative and formative," all these functions being able, if unchecked, to drive a man crazy.

After all that, one single stanza is enough to describe the process of reawakening. He wants to continue with his will, but in the meantime his ink has frozen and his candle has gone out. He has no fire to relight it, and so he goes to bed all wrapped up.

All forty stanzas of the "Legacy" have the same form, eight lines of eight syllables with the rimes a b a b b c b c. For the most part each stanza forms a unit complete in itself. Only rarely are two connected, three in the case of the scholastic verbiage.

In older editions, the "Legacy" is sometimes named the "Little Testament," and then what Villon called merely the "Testament" will be distinguished as the "Great Testament." This change of Villon's own title must have been made early, for he himself complained about it in stanza 75 of the Testament:

> Si me souvient bien, Dieu mercis,
> Que je feis a mon partement
> Certains laiz, l'an cinquante six,
> Qu'aucuns, sans mon consentement,
> Voulurent nommer Testament;
> Leur plaisir fut, non pas le myen.
> Mais quoy? on dit communement
> Qu'ung chascun n'est maistre du sien.

> (I remember well, praise God,
> That I composed on my departure
> Certain legacies, in 'fifty-six,
> Which some, with no consent of mine,
> Have wished to call a Testament;
> The wish was theirs, not mine.
> But so what? They say
> No man is master of his own.) (B)

So he wanted the title "Testament" to apply exclusively to his later and longer work. In calling the earlier work "Les Lais" ("Legacy") and the later one simply the "Testament," modern editors actually comply with the poet's own wish.

CHAPTER 5

Villon's "Testament"

IF Villon had died in the dungeon of Meung, as he very well might have, he would never have been rated a great poet. Perhaps a few of the *ballades* he had written earlier would have been preserved along with the "Legacy"; but we should have none of the truly great ones, and he would never have written the "Testament."

The underlying idea of the "Testament" is the same as that of the "Legacy," since it likewise purports to be a will. The difference, nevertheless, is enormous.

Villon says very little about himself in the "Legacy." The entire introduction, in which he presents himself as a disillusioned lover, is pure fiction. He allows us a glimpse at himself in the stanza where he tells of hearing the bell of the Sorbonne, and again, after the mock-scholastic passage, when he finds his ink frozen and his candle blown out. That is all. To be sure, assiduous scholars might learn a little more about him by finding out who his friends were, but the lines themselves tell nothing.

But back in Paris, after five years of hardships and a summer of intense suffering, he begins:

> En l'an de mon trentiesme aage,
> Que toutes mes hontes j'eus beues . . .
>
> (In the thirtieth year of my life,
> when I had drunk all my degradations . . .)

He cannot hold his feelings back. They burst forth. In stanza after stanza he cries out to the world, spreads out his sentiments and thoughts, his doubts and hopes. The "Legacy" consisted of forty stanzas in all. In the "Testament" there are eighty-four stanzas before he even begins bequeathing. Furthermore, wherever the thought expressed established a connection, he inserted into the "Testament" independent poems, namely sixteen *ballades,* one *chanson* or *bergeronnette,* two *rondeaux,* and finally two poems in the same type of stanzas as the "Testament," but clearly distinct from it. The "Testament" itself consists of 186 stanzas.

I *His Hatred of Bishop Thibaud d'Aussigny*

In the thirtieth year of my life, when I had drunk all my degradations, neither altogether a fool nor altogether wise, in spite of many a torment received which were all inflicted by Thibaut d'Aussigny . . . Though he is a bishop who may bless the streets, I deny that he is mine.

He is neither my lord nor my bishop. I hold no land from him except what is fallow. I do not owe him homage. I am neither his serf nor his doe [this is a pun: the words "serf" and "cerf" are pronounced alike, and cerf means "stag"]. All he ever gave me was a little bit of bread and cold water for a whole summer! Whether he normally is generous or stingy, to me he has been most miserly. May God be to him what he was to me!

He continues on that theme. No, he is not cursing the bishop; he fervently prays that God may treat the bishop as the bishop treated him.

He knows well that one should pray for one's enemies, and that is what he does. Indeed he will compose for the bishop a nice Picard's prayer; if he does not understand it, let him go to Douai or Lille and learn Picard!

This is, of course, another pun. Picards was the current French name for one branch of the Hussite heretics who rejected the use of prayer, but Picards are also the people of Picardie, which was then a part of Burgundian Flanders.

"And if he wants a different kind of prayer, let him look up the 108th Psalm, verse 7" ["Let his days be few and let another take his office"].

II   *His Praise of the King*

Here for a time his invectives against the bishop are interrupted, and he now praises the king who freed him from that cruel power. May he have all the good fortune of Jacob, the honor and glory of Solomon, and may he live as long as Methuselah.

It is doubtful whether Louis XI would have appreciated it if Villon's next wish had come true: may he have twelve children, all male. The concluding line, though, wishes him the joys of Paradise.

At this point Villon makes a move toward writing his will, but other thoughts force themselves upon him. He feels that suffering has made him wiser and more mature.

It is true that after complaints and tears and anguished moans, after despair and pains, hardships and sad wanderings, my mind that had been rubbed smooth as a billiard ball was opened up by sufferings more than by all of Averroes' commentaries on Aristotle.

And indeed, when my misery was at its worst and I walked on the road without a penny, God, who according to the Gospel comforted the pilgrims at Emmaus, showed me a good town that was equipped with the gift of hope.

Hope—*Espérance*—was the slogan of the dukes of Bourbon, and Moulins was the town in question. Among the poems not included in the "Testament" is one addressed to the duke of Bourbon. Villon wittily asks him for a little loan of money in a tone that indicates previous acquaintance and takes a friendly disposition for granted. So this stanza makes it seem probable that at some time during those wanderings

Villon was well treated by that noble lord. But this is only a reminiscence, and the stanza continues:

However vile a sinner may be, the only thing God hates is persistence in sin.

I am a sinner, I know it well, but God does not wish my death. He would rather see me converted and leading a good life, me and all the others whom sin has bitten. Although I may be dead in sin, God lives, and if my conscience makes me repent, He will grant me pardon by His grace.

It says in the noble Romance of the Rose that old people must forgive a young heart when they see it in its youthfulness. That is so true: Yet those who harass me so do not even want me to reach maturity.

If my death could in any way be of advantage to the common good, I would condemn myself to death, so help me God! I will not complain to young or old, whether I am on my feet or in the grave. For a poor man the mountains will move neither forward nor backward.

III   *Alexander and the Pirate*

Here follows a little story about a pirate who was brought in chains before Alexander.

"Why are you a pirate?" the king asks him.

"I am now called a pirate because I have only one little ship to operate with. If I had a whole fleet like you I would also be an emperor. But I was poor, and fortune was against me. She cast my dice unfavorably. There is a common saying that in great poverty there is no great respect for the law."

Alexander was impressed with those words and so, instead of executing him, he gave the pirate the means to become a worthy man. And, indeed, the former pirate became a great man.

Thus now the trend of thought is on bad luck, that poverty especially is the cause of iniquity, just as hunger forces the wolf to attack people.

IV *Regrets about Youth Gone and Wasted*

O how I regret the days of my youth. I did have a good time then, but youth left me without announcing its departure. It did not leave me on foot, and not on horseback either. It just suddenly was not there any more. So it is gone, and I remain here, poor in sense and in knowledge, sad, cheated, blacker than a mulberry. I draw no interest nor rent, I have nothing. My relatives disown me, forgetting their natural duty, just on account of a slight lack of capital.

Poverty and lost youth remain the theme through several stanzas. Then comes a more definite regret:

God! if I had studied in the days of my foolish youth, and had formed good habits, I would now have a house and a soft bed. But what? I avoided school like a bad boy. As I write down these words, it nearly tears my heart in two.

Even in studying Ecclesiastes he heeded only half of the lesson. Where it says, "Have a good time, my son, in your adolescence," he did not continue reading to where it says: "Youth and adolescence are nothing but vice and ignorance." Now his days of youthfulness are gone. He does not fear fate any more, for death will settle everything. Death is now the main theme.

Where are all those pleasant buddies I went with in the old days? They sang so well, they talked so well, they were so pleasing in all they did and said. Well, some are dead and stiff now; there is nothing left of them. May they rest in Paradise, and may God save the others! Of these, some, thank God, have become great lords and masters, others beg naked and see bread only through windows. Others again have become monks, Celestines and Carthusians, and wear better shoes and hose than you would expect.

As for them who have become great masters, God grant them to do right and to live in peace. In their case nothing needs to be corrected, but may God grant patience to the poor who have nothing, like myself. The others do not lack anything. They have bread and regular rations.

They have good wines, often fresh from the cask, sauces, soup, fat fish, pies, custard; their eggs are fried, poached, scrambled, served in any style. Their food and drink is not rationed out as it is to stone masons. They don't need waiters: they pour it themselves.

At this point, stanza 33, the poet realizes that he has been carried away by his feelings.

What got me into this digression is my poverty. Poverty makes a man bilious and satirical. If poverty does not say a biting word outright it still thinks it.

I have always been poor, of poor and humble extraction. My father never had any wealth, nor had his grandfather, whose name was Horace. Poverty had followed and tracked us all. On the tombs of my ancestors there are no sceptres nor crowns.

Yet when I complain about poverty my heart often tells me: "Do not grieve so much. What good did it do Jacques Coeur to possess so much? Is it not better to be alive, even in coarse clothes, than to be rotting in a rich grave?"

Now the theme is the death dance:

> No I'm not, I'm well aware
> an angel's son with diadem
> of stars and constellations.
> My father's dead, God rest his soul,
> his body lying under gravestone.
> They say my mother too will die
> (the poor old woman knows it well),
> and the son will not be long.

> I know that rich and poor,
> fools and wisemen, priests and laymen,
> nobles, peasants, princes and misers,
> small and large, fair and ugly,
> ladies with upturned collars,
> and of any class whatever, wearing

costly hats or simple bonnets,
Death seizes without exception.

Paris dies, and Helen too;
whoever dies, dies in pain
such that breath fails him:
his spleen bursts upon his heart,
he sweats—good God, what sweat!—
and no one can relieve him in his agony;
for he has no brother, child or sister
who at that moment wants to take his place.

Death makes him tremble and turn white,
curls his nostrils, stretches taut his veins,
puffs out his neck, makes flesh turn flabby,
joints and nerves dilate and swell.
O woman's body, so tender,
smooth, soft and precious,
do these ills await you too?
Yes, unless you go alive to heaven. (B)

V *The Ladies of Bygone Days*

Death taking away lovely women—that was the ideal
place for inserting a *ballade* he had probably composed much
earlier. This *ballade* asking about the ladies of bygone days
is one of the best known of his poems. If nothing so far had
revealed Villon as a true poet, this *ballade* certainly would.

To give an impression of the poetic form, this *ballade*
must be presented in the original.

Dictes moy ou, n'en quel pays,
Est Flora, la belle Rommaine,
Archipiades, ne Thaïs
Qui fut sa cousine germaine,
Echo parlant quant bruyt on maine
Dessus riviere ou sus estan,
Qui beaulté ot trop plus qu'humaine.
Mais ou sont les neiges d'antan?

Ou est la tres sage Hellois
Pour qui fut chastré et puis moyne
Pierre Esbaillard a Saint Denis?
Pour son amour ot ceste essoyne.
Semblablement, ou est la royne
Qui commanda que Buridan
Fust geté en ung sac en Seine?
Mais ou sont les neiges d'antan?

La royne Blanche comme lis
Qui chantoit a voix de seraine,
Berte au grand pié, Biétris, Alis,
Haremburgis qui tint le Maine,
Et Jehanne la bonne Lorraine
Qu'Englois brulerent a Rouan;
Ou sont ilz, ou, Vierge souvraine?
Mais ou sont les neiges d'antan?

Prince, n'enquerrez de sepmaine
Ou elles sont, ne de cest an,
Que ce refrain ne vous remaine:
Mais ou sont les neiges d'antan?

(Tell me where, and in what country, is Flora, the beautiful
Roman, Archipiades and Thais who was her first cousin, Echo,
who talks when noise is made near a river or a pond, she who
had more than human beauty. But where are last year's snows?

Where is the very learned Heloise for whose sake Peter
Abelard was castrated and had to be a monk in Saint Denis—
he suffered this misfortune for having loved her? Similarly, where
is the queen who ordered Buridan to be thrown into the Seine
in a sack? But where are last year's snows?

Queen Blanche, [white] as a lily, who sang with a siren's
voice, Bigfooted Bertha, Beatrice, Alice, Haremburgis who ruled
over Maine, and Jeanne, the good girl from Lorraine, whom the
English burned at Rouen—where are they, where, sovereign
Virgin? But where are last year's snows?

Prince, do not try to find out this week where they are, nor this year. Let this refrain stay with you: Where are last year's snows.)

Again, form and theme are conventional. There are many such poetic enumerations, listing a number of persons who have something in common. Here it is the sad fact that they all have disappeared like last year's snow. Much of the indescribable charm of this poem lies in that refrain: "Mais où sont les neiges d'antan?"

To mention a point of external poetic form, this refrain also stands out for its extraordinary rhythm. In lines of eight syllables such as these, the caesura or stop usually comes in the middle or divides the line either 3+5 or 5+3. In the refrain the strongest word is *où*, and the natural break in the line therefore comes after the second syllable, which results in the very rare division 2+6.

VI *Identification of Characters*

But who are those ladies? Flora, the beautiful Roman, is described by Juvenal as one who enslaves men with her great charms. The second one, Archipiades, is a strange case. In the books accessible to medieval students, notably in Boetius, reference is made to "beautiful" Alcibiades. In other texts Alcibiades is presented as the darling of the leading men in Athens. It was known that Socrates had been in love with Alcibiades. Although homosexuality existed and was even one of the prevalent "vices" in monasteries and in the military monastic orders, such unashamed references to it as an accepted thing were incomprehensible to the medieval mind. Alcibiades must have been a lovely lady, another of the famous courtesans of antiquity, like Thais, the "hetaera" who charmed the great Alexander. The two must have resembled each other like first cousins.

Echo is the only mythological figure on Villon's list. She who had "more than human beauty" was also extremely talkative, and her incessant chatter exasperated Hera-Juno, the stern goddess who had much cause to be jealous of pretty women. So she was reduced to a mere echo "who talks when noise is made near a river or a pond."

So much for antiquity. In the second stanza the poet turns to women of more recent times. Héloise was indeed very learned. At the age of fifteen she had mastered all the liberal arts to the point of being able to take part in any discussion. She must have been very attractive, too, for a man like Abelard to risk his promising career—he had good prospects of becoming pope—by letting himself become hopelessly involved with her. Punishment came swiftly. When it became known that Héloise had become pregnant, her relatives overpowered and castrated the great philosopher. This put an end to his ambitions, for in the Western church, in contrast to the Eastern, no eunuch could hold a high ecclesiastical office.

As for the queen mentioned next, she actually existed and may have done the things with which she is credited, except that she could not possibly have had an affair with Buridan who was only five years old at the time of her death. She was Jeanne of Navarre, wife of Philip the Fair. The story is that she had a love nest in the Tour de Nesles on the bank of the Seine. There she kept many a lover for a number of happy days, but then, to safeguard her reputation, she had them put in sacks and thrown through the window into the river. Buridan, a philosopher of note and a professor at the university, was extremely popular with his students and was therefore well remembered. In Villon's days, not quite a century later, several legends about him were current. One was that, greatly alarmed by the mysterious disappearance of a number of students, he decided to investigate the matter. He had heard rumors about the queen, and so he carried his detective work to the point of becoming the queen's lover. He enjoyed it royally, but when the time came for him to be tossed out, there was a barge full of hay ready to receive him. The students who maneuvered the barge threw a large rock into the river to produce the expected splash.

The last stanza first inquires about historical and semi-legendary ladies. Blanche was the mother of Saint Louis, "La royne Blanche comme lys." Since *blanche* means white, the word does not have to be repeated to make her white as a lily. Bigfooted Bertha, the mother of Charlemagne, was well known from the *Chanson de Geste,* and so were the ladies Beatrice and Alice. As for Arembourg, she was the heiress and countess regnant of Maine until the infamous Foulque of Anjou forced her to marry him, then cruelly murdered her a little later.

But right after the reference to that rather obscure eleventh-century countess come the stirring lines:

> And Jeanne, the good girl from Lorraine,
> whom the English burned at Rouen.

Here the intensity of the feeling strikes through the poorest of translations. It may well be that these two lines are the origin of that strange image of Villon as the great patriot.

On the whole, this *ballade* has inexplicable charm. Technically it is not one of Villon's best. The *envoi* is rather weak. The enumeration of classical, historical, and legendary women is haphazard. There are other weaknesses, but they in no way affect the intangible beauty of the poem.

The incomparable charm of this *ballade* becomes even more evident in contrast with the other two enumerating *ballades* which follow.

The first enumerates popes, kings, and other famous men who, for the most part, had died only a few years before. Du Guesclin, the great military leader, is the only one who belongs to the previous century, and the refrain is: "But where is great Charlemagne?"

The second, likewise an enumeration of famous men, has the distinction of being written in imitation Old French.

Villon did not know the language of three centuries earlier. The remnants of a noun declension, such as the distinction between *li roys,* subject, and *le roy,* object, were unknown to him. So he haphazardly replaced *le* by *li* and added *s* to singular nouns, regardless of case. The enumeration is even more tedious than the preceding one. Only the refrain clings to one's memory: "Autant en emporte le vent." And when Margaret Mitchell's novel was published in France, this refrain was chosen as French title of *Gone with the Wind.*

The fact remains that the two *ballades* about departed men are tedious, whereas the one about departed women is utterly charming. While the difference is spontaneously felt, it would be extremely hard to analyze.

VII   Ballade *Form and Example from Swinburne*

It may be in order here to explain the term *ballade.* Like all other medieval names for types of poems, it refers primarily to the arrangement of the rimes. From the very beginning, the Troubadours of southern France developed the most elaborate rime-schemes, and for each one they had a name. Best known to the average English reader may be the Petrarchan sonnet, a late outgrowth of this care for regularly arranged rimes. Edna St. Vincent Millay was one of the last poets to use this form with mastery.

The *ballade,* then, is a poem in which the same alternating rimes go through three stanzas and a shorter stanza called *envoi.* But rather than describe abstractly what is primarily a matter of the ear, I shall give here as an example the *ballade* Swinburne wrote in homage to Villon. Whatever we may think of the style and of the sentiments expressed, it is one of the most perfect examples to illustrate the form.[7]

> Bird of the bitter bright grey golden morn
> Scarce risen upon the dusk of dolorous years,
> First of us all and sweetest singer born

Whose far shrill note the world of new men hears
Cleave the cold shuddering shade as twilight clears;
When song new-born put off the old world's attire
And felt its tune on her changed lips expire,
Writ foremost on the roll of them that came
Fresh girt for service of the latter lyre,
Villon, our sad bad glad mad brother's name!

Alas the joy, the sorrow and the scorn,
That clothed thy life with hopes and sins and fears,
And gave thee stones for bread and tares for corn
And plume-plucked gad-birds for thy starveling peers
Till death clipt close their flight with shameful shears;
Till shifts came short and loves were hard to hire,
When lilt of song nor twitch of twangling wire
Could buy thee bread or kisses; when light fame
Spurned like a ball and haled through brake and briar,
Villon, our sad bad glad mad brother's name!

Poor splendid wings so frayed and soiled and torn!
Poor kind wild eyes so dashed with light quick tears!
Poor perfect voice, most blithe when most forlorn,
That rings athwart the sea whence no man steers
Like joy-bells crossed with death-bells in our ears!
What far delight has cooled the fierce desire
That like some ravenous bird was strong to tire
On that frail flesh and soul consumed with flame,
But left more sweet than roses to respire,
Villon, our sad bad glad mad brother's name?

ENVOI

Prince of sweet songs made out of tears and fire,
A harlot was thy nurse, a God thy sire;
Shame soiled thy song, and song assoiled thy shame,
But from thy feet now death has washed the mire,
Love reads out first at head of all our quire,
Villon, our sad bad glad mad brother's name.

This work of Swinburne shows how the rimes repeat themselves throughout the poem and again in the shorter *envoi.*

The word *envoi* means "send-off." The first *ballades,* no
doubt, were transmitted by word of mouth; the minstrel
was sent by the poet to recite the poem to some high noble.
Very soon the tradition developed that the *envoi* had to
begin with the word "Prince," a convention no longer
rigidly adhered to in Villon's day. Of the sixteen *ballades*
included in the "Testament," nine *envois* begin with the
word Prince (one with the variant Princesse), and seven
without it.

VIII *The Old Women*

After his *ballade* in faulty Old French, Villon resumes his
musings on the finality of death and the treacherous surprise
attack of old age. If a man is so poor that he has to beg
and feels old age taking possession of him, he will reach
the point where, "if it were not for the fear of God, he
would commit a terrible deed" by putting an end to his
life. For in old age there is nothing to enjoy any more. An
old monkey can please no one, and if he makes the faces
that used to be funny, he is now only repulsive. If an old
man keeps silent, people say he is senile; if he talks, they
tell him to keep quiet.

Even more to be pitied are old women who are destitute.
They see young girls assuming charge and they ask God
why he caused them to be born so early. Our Lord does
not answer; He knows He would lose the argument.

At this point, Villon remembers a real person, the one
who used to be called "the beautiful Armorer" (helmet-
maker). He had seen her hang around the taverns, a poor
old hag of eighty or more. O, she had had her good days,
but that had been long before Villon was born. She had
been the mistress of a very wealthy and influential church-
man, Nicolas d'Orgemont, the archdeacon at Notre Dame.
He had openly installed her in the canons' cloister and had

fitted her out like a queen. She was a public figure for her beauty and elegance. In 1416, however, all this had abruptly ended. When her lover became involved in a plot against the insane king, Charles VI, he was sentenced to life imprisonment and his entire fortune was confiscated. For her, this meant a complete downfall. For a while she attached herself—too much, she complains—to a pimp and sold her declining charms. Now she drags herself from tavern to tavern, begging for the wine that will warm her blood and an occasional crust of bread. She presents a horrible picture of misery and decrepitude. This ghastly picture now appears before Villon, and he thinks he can hear her express her regrets:

You sneaky fierce old age, why have you struck me down so soon? Who would cherish me so much to keep me from killing myself?

You have taken from me the great power which beauty had given me over clerics, merchants, and churchmen, for then there was no man who would not have given me—although he might later have been sorry for it—everything he had in exchange for that which now even the vilest beggars would refuse to take.

I refused that to many a man—that was silly of me—because I was in love with a sly fellow to whom I gave it generously. O, I occasionally deceived him just a little, but, by my soul, I loved him. He was rough with me and loved me only for what I had to give.

He could have dragged me through the mud and trampled me —I still would have loved him. Even if he had kicked my kidneys out of place and then asked me to kiss him, I would have forgotten all my woes. That vice-stained glutton kissed me. . . . A lot of good it has done me! What have I got now? Shame and sin!

But he died some thirty years ago, and I have stayed behind, old and gray. When I think, alas, of the old days, what a person I was, and what I have become! When I look at myself naked and see myself so much changed, poor, dried up, emaciated, shrivelled, I nearly go mad with rage.

What has become of my smooth forehead. . . .

She goes on, describing her body as it used to be. She does not leave out a single detail. Then comes the contrast:

The forehead wrinkled, the hair gray, the eyebrows fallen out, the eyes without lustre . . ." and she describes her poor repulsive body with the same detailed care as she had her youthful charms: shoulders, breasts, etc., and the thighs are now all shrivelled-up and spotted like sausages.

Thus we poor old fools now regret the good times amongst ourselves, when we squat together like a ball of wool close to a miserable little fire of hemp stalks which (like ourselves) catch fire so quickly and go out so soon. And to think how pretty we once were! Yet this will happen to all, men and women alike.

This independent poem on the regrets of the once beautiful Armorer's wife is not cast in *ballade* form, but is written in the same stanzas of eight lines each as the "Testament" itself.

It is followed by a *ballade* in which the old woman admonishes the young ones, telling them to take full advantage of their youth.

Now do some thinking, pretty Glover, who used to be my pupil, and you, Blanche the Slipper-Maker, it is time for you to know yourselves. Take right and left, don't spare a single man, for once you are old, you will be worth nothing, like money that has been taken out of circulation.

And you, sweet Sausage-Maker who can dance so well, Guillemette the Tapestry-Maker, don't shortchange your master, or else you will have to close your shop. Once you have become old, ugly, you will be able only to serve some old priest, like money that has been taken out of circulation.

Jeanneton the Hat-Maker, don't let your friend enslave you, and Katherine the Purse-Maker, don't send men away any more. Even one who is not so pretty should not be awkward, but should smile at them. Ugly old age cannot hold love; it is like money that has been taken out of circulation.

Envoi: Girls, get busy, and understand why I now cry and moan. It is because I have become so useless as money that has been taken out of circulation.

Villon is careful to state that these are the old woman's ideas, not his own. Let us pretend we believe him when he says:

I have had those admonishments of the old woman taken down by my scatterbrained clerk Fremin who has about as much sense as I have. If he says it was not so, I will curse him, for masters are being judged by what their clerks are.

The scholars fairly well agree that the clerk Fremin, who will be mentioned in a few more places, is pure fiction.

IX *Women in General*

Villon's thoughts are still on women. He realizes how dangerous they can be to a man who would love them. (But surely some moralist would tell Villon that he should not draw general conclusions from the behavior of the women he knows, for they are all disreputable.)

If they love only for the money, one should love them but for an hour. They simply love everybody and laugh when your purse weeps. Of those there is not one who would not be after something. A decent man, so help me God, should devote himself only to women of honor and reputation, not elsewhere.

If I hear somebody talking like this, it does not give me any satisfaction. In fact, what he is driving at—and I think I understand him well—is that one should love only where it is proper. What I would like to know is whether the girls I talk to all day long have ever been honest women.

Truly they were once honest, without deserving reproach or blame. It is true that in the beginning everyone of those women, before they became disreputable, took, the one a clerk, the other a layman, still another a monk, to put out the flames of love which are hotter than Saint Anthony's fire.

They acted according to the decree: they loved their friends—this is evident—in some secret place, and nobody else had a part in it. But, as you know, love has to be shared, and she who loved only one man moves away from him and leaves; she prefers to love everybody.

What makes them do that? Without intending any criticism, I believe that it is simply feminine nature that makes them wish to love in such a lively manner. I have no other explanation, unless it is what is commonly said in Rheims and Troyes, in fact also in Lille and in St. Omer, that six workers accomplish more than three.

So the foolish lovers are bounced out, and the ladies go their way; this is the proper reward lovers get: every faith is violated, however sweet the kiss and the embrace. "In the case of hounds, falcons, war, love," that's what everybody says everywhere, "for one pleasure there are a thousand woes."

Here follows a *double ballade*. It differs from the simple one only in that it has six stanzas and no *envoi*. The rimes are repeated as in the simple *ballade*. The theme is the bad consequences of love. It is a jumble of examples taken from legend and history. The refrain is: "He is lucky who has nothing."

Solomon worshipped idols for the sake of his women; Orpheus, playing the flute and the bagpipe, had to face Cerberus, the frightful dog with four [not three] heads; Narcissus drowned himself; an unexplained Sardana, who conquered Crete, wanted to be changed into a woman; David, the pious king, forgot the fear of God when he saw a pair of well-shaped thighs being washed; Amon, pretending to have a craving for cakes, raped his sister Tamar; Herod had John the Baptist's head cut off to see a woman dance.

Thus far it is all mythology, Bible, and legend; but now the poet can no longer speak of others.

Now I must speak of my own poor self. I got a beating like laundry being thrashed in a stream; all naked I was, I will not keep it a secret. And who made me chew those gooseberries? Who but Katherine de Vausselles. Noel was the third man present. Mittens at the wedding did I get. He is lucky who has nothing.

"Mittens at the wedding," which is found also in Rabelais, is a humorous euphemism for a beating. It is obviously a reference to some crude old wedding custom. As for Katherine de Vausselles, she remains a mystery in spite of all scholarly efforts made on her account. The imaginative biographers have taken full advantage of this name and of the total absence of any further information.

The *double ballade* concludes:

But do not expect this young bachelor [of arts] to leave the bacheloresses alone. No, even if he were to be burned alive like the people who ride on brooms, they are sweeter to him than civet perfume. Just the same it takes a fool to trust them, be they white (blonde) or brunettes. He is lucky who has nothing.

"Bacheloresses" (in French, *bachelettes* or *bachelières*) is a humorous word coined by students.

Villon now recalls how the girl he once loved mastered the art of fooling him. O, she would listen to him without agreeing or disagreeing, but then she would tell him things that were amusing enough but never true. She would always make him believe that one thing was another, that flour was ashes, that a rimless cap was a felt hat, that some rusty old iron was pewter, that deuces were aces (this only renders the idea); a cheater always fools somebody and sells bladders for lanterns. Of the sky she made a copper frying pan, of the clouds a calfskin, of morning she made evening, of a cabbage stalk a turnip, of cheap beer new wine, of a sow a windmill, of a hangman's noose a skein of yarn, of a fat abbot a squire.

This is how love made a fool of me, and led me from the door to the latch. I do not believe there is any man smart enough, with wits as fine as pure silver, who would not lose his shirt and clothes and even be handled as I was, I who openly call myself the rejected, dismissed lover.

So he renounces love forever and curses it, and if anybody should say, "How dare you?" he would answer that a dying man has a right to say anything.

The next stanza is pathetic:

> I feel my thirst approaching:
> I spit gobs of phlegm as white
> as cotton and as big as tennis balls.
> What is there to say? That Jeanneton
> no longer takes me for a youth,
> but for an ancient, worn-out hack
> Already my voice is old and cracked,
> and here I am still young and green. (B)

X *The Bishop Again*

What has made such a wreck of him is that imprisonment in Meung. And so he goes again. He calls the bishop Tacque Thibaud, who was a much detested man guilty of many acts of violence and oppression, playing on the bishop's first name. He continues:

> he who made me drink so much cold water,
> having put me in a low place, not a high one,
> made me eat many an anguish pear,
> in irons. . . . When I remember it
> I pray for him—*et reliqua* [and the rest]—
> May God give him, truly, truly,
> what I think—*et cetera.*

The "anguish pear" was an instrument of torture that was put into the victim's mouth and then expanded to hurt his jaws and choke him. Villon then also refers with biting mock kindness to his other tormentors, the bishop's lieutenant, his official, and maître Robert, the hangman of Orléans. He loves them all as God loves money changers.

After these last powerful invectives he remembers the "Legacy" he made in 1456, and that some people, without his consent, have named that work "Testament." The stanza has been quoted before.

Villon will not revoke any of his bequests. If anyone has not received what he was promised, he should ask Villon's heirs; he names three tavern keepers to whom he probably still owes money.

He would like to start on his will—he had such good laughs with it back in 1456—and yet he cannot get into the mood. There are too many other things in him, things that had never before been put into writing by anyone either in verse or prose. Writing such things down violated every known literary standard. When had a poet or prose writer ever expressed feelings that were uniquely his own, feelings that had not been classified and labeled before? It just was not done. Yet he, otherwise so strict in all matters of literary form, was simply unable to refrain from saying what his poor heart could not hold back. Thus the original plan to write a mock will is constantly crossed either by violent outpourings of feelings or by musings based on entirely personal experience.

On the other hand, many an expression that will appear extremely original to the modern reader was not new at all. So Villon's tendency to use burlesque phrases in reference to religious matters was almost commonplace, because that was the way the Dominicans preached to reach the minds of the untutored. An example of this comes right after the invocation of Holy Trinity. He speaks of the many who had died and were doomed since the days of Adam, and then adds:

> . . . their bodies rotten, their souls in flames
> no matter what had been their state before.

I make exception, though,
of all the patriarchs and prophets
who, as I see things,
never had their buttocks overheated. (B)

After a reference, in similar popular tone, to the parable
Lazarus and the rich man, Villon at last begins.

XI *Bequests*

He leaves his soul to God and his body to Mother Earth.
Then:

Furthermore, to my more than father, maître Guillaume de
Villon, who has been kinder to me than a mother is to an infant
child; he got me out of many a mess, but is not too happy about
the present one; therefore, I beg him on my knees to leave the
whole joy of it to me; I leave him my books, including the novel
Pet au Diable which maître Guy Tabarie, a most reliable man,
copied. It is in notebooks under the table.

Next is his mother. He has nothing to give her, nothing
material. But as the poor old woman, who has suffered so
much sorrow and grief on his account, gets all her comfort
from her trust in the Holy Virgin, he will give her a prayer
in form of a *ballade*, a prayer she will be able to recite at
the altar. The original is too stirringly beautiful to be left
out here.

Dame du ciel, regente terrienne,
Emperiere des infernaux palus,
Recevez moy, vostre humble chrestienne,
Que comprinse soye entre vos esleus,
Ce non obstant qu'oncques rien ne valus.
Les biens de vous, Ma Dame et Ma Maistresse
Sont trop plus grans que ne suis pecheresse,
Sans lesquels biens ame ne peut merir
N'avoir les cieulx. Je n'en suis jangleresse:
En ceste foy je vueil vivre et mourir.

A vostre Filz dictes que je suis sienne;
De luy soyent mes pechiez abolus;
Pardonne moy comme a l'Egipcienne,
Ou comme il feist au clerc Theophilus,
Lequel par vous fut quitte et absolus,
Combien qu'il eust au deable fait promesse
Preservez moy de ne faire jamais ce,
Vierge portant, sans rompure encourir,
Le sacrement qu'on celebre a la messe.
En ceste foy je vueil vivre et mourir.

Femme je suis povrette et ancïenne,
Qui riens ne sçay; oncques lettre ne leus.
Au moustier voy dont suis paroissienne
Paradis paint, ou sont harpes et lus,
Et ung enfer ou dampnez sont boullus:
L'ung me fait paour, l'autre joye et liesse.
La joye avoir me fay, haulte Deesse,
A qui pecheurs doivent tous recourir,
Comblez de foy, sans fainte ne paresse.
En ceste foy je vueil vivre et mourir.

Vous portastes, digne Vierge, princesse,
Iesus regnant qui n'a ne fin ne cesse.
Le Tout Puissant, prenant nostre foiblesse,
Laissa les cieulx et nous vint secourir,
Offrit a mort sa tres chiere jeunesse;
Nostre Seigneur tel est, tel le confesse.
En ceste foy je vueil vivre et mourir.

(Lady of the Heavens, ruler of the earth, empress of the infernal marshes, receive me, your humble Christian, that I may be included among your chosen ones, although I was never worth anything. Your gifts, my Lady and my Mistress, very much outweigh my sins. Without these gifts no soul can have merit nor have heavenly bliss. I am not speaking lightly: In this faith I wish to live and die.

Tell your Son that I am His. Let my sins be washed off by Him; may He pardon me as He did the Egyptian, or as He did the clerk Theophilus who was acquitted and absolved by your intercession although he had promised his soul to the devil. Keep me from ever doing a thing like that, you who, without suffering a break of your virginity, bore the sacrament that is celebrated at Mass. In this faith I wish to live and die.

I am a poor old woman who knows nothing; I never learned to read. In the church, whose parishioner I am, I can see painted a paradise, where there are harps and lutes, and a hell where the damned are being boiled: the one frightens me, and the other gives me gladness and joy. Make me have the joy, lofty goddess, whose intercession all sinners must seek; fill me with faith without hypocrisy or lack of zeal. In this faith I wish to live and die.

You, worthy Virgin, princess, bore Jesus whose reign is without term or end. The Almighty, assuming our feebleness, left the heavens and came to our aid, offered His dear young body to death. He is our Lord, so I testify. In this faith I wish to live and die.)

This prayer the poor old woman could now learn by heart and recite, and perhaps the Holy Virgin would know that he, Villon, was also included, though modestly hidden in the acrostic of the *envoi*.

To continue in so deeply sincere a tone would not have been possible. He had to wipe the tears from his eyes and overcome this wave of emotion. That was best done by turning from his mother to his Rose, that is to say, to the woman whose name is given in acrostic as Marthe, because then he could play with invented conventional feelings and top the invention with crude cynicism. He well knows that she would rather be left a purse full of money than receive his heart, but let him be hanged who would leave her a single coin! She has enough anyhow, and at any rate he does not care. His love sufferings are over; his tail no longer burns. He leaves Rose to the descendants of him who was named "the Good Fornicator." But although he owes the woman nothing, he owes Love a token of homage. So he will send Rose a *ballade*.

I will send her this *ballade* whose every line ends in R. Who will bring it to her? O yes, I see, it will be Pernet de la Barre [this man was known for his sexual accomplishments], provided that, when he encounters on his way my lady with the upturned nose, he greet her, without further politeness, with the words: "You filthy whore, where have you been!"

There, this writer believes, goes the image of Villon, the Romantic lover! If the *ballade* did not have this preface, perhaps it might have fooled someone.

False beauty, who has cost me so dearly, harsh in fact, with hypocritical sweetness, a love harder to chew than iron, whom, in the certain expectation of my undoing, I may call a felon charm, the death of my heart, a hidden pride that will send men to their death, eyes without pity. Will not Justice help a poor man without making things worse?

It would have been better had I looked for help elsewhere. It would have saved my honor; then nothing would have had me hacked to pieces on account of that. Now I must run away in flight and dishonor. Help, help! great and lowly! And what is it? Shall I die without striking back? Or will Pity, moved by these tones, help a poor man without making things worse?

There will be a time that will cause your open flower to dry up, to turn yellow and wilt. Then I will laugh if I still have teeth with which to laugh; but no, that would be silly. I shall be old; you, ugly, without color. So drink as long as the stream runs; do not give everyone such suffering. Help a poor man without making things worse.

Prince in love, of all lovers the greatest, I would not risk to be on bad terms with you, but every decent heart must, for the sake of Our Lord, help a poor man without making things worse!

For all its formal perfection—in the first stanza the acrostic reads Françoys; in the second, Marthe—this *ballade* is one of the weakest. The conventional verbiage is almost impenetrable, and yet all these many words do not convey a single idea that had not been hashed and rehashed all over Europe for more than three centuries. Furthermore the refrain is not directly understandable.

The next on his list is Ythier Marchant, who in the Legacy had been given something that could just as well have been a sword or a piece of feces. He was a constable, but fortunately a corrupt one, and the poet was on good terms with him. So this time, knowing that the constable recently lost in death a woman of whom he was fond, Villon sends him a pretty *rondeau* and advises him to set it to music. Marchant was not a composer, but evidently he found a competent one, for a copy of this poem, with music for two accompanying instruments, has been preserved.

> Mort, j'appelle de ta rigueur,
> Qui m'as ma maistresse ravie,
> Et n'es pas encore assouvie
> Si tu ne me tiens en langueur:
> Onc puis n'eus force ne vigueur;
> Mais que te nuysoit elle en vie?
> Mort, j'appelle de ta rigueur,
> Qui m'as ma maistresse ravie.
>
> Deux estions et n'avions qu'ung cuer;
> S'il est mort, force est que je devie,
> Voire, ou que je vive sans vie
> Comme les images, par cuer.
> Mort, j'appelle de ta rigueur,
> Qui m'as ma maistresse ravie.

(Death, I appeal against your harshness, for having taken my mistress away from me, and you are still not satisfied if you cannot hold me in a state of dejection. Since then I have had no strength or vigor. But what harm did she do you when she was alive? Death, I appeal against your harshness, for having taken my mistress away from me.

We were two, and yet we had only one heart. If it is dead, I too will have to die, indeed, or live without life, like an image, in appearance only. Death, I appeal against your harshness, for having taken my mistress away from me.)

Now come the various bequests, in the same manner as in the "Legacy," but most of the wit and the humor is totally lost to us. He is very generous with worthless gifts and with shop signs. To Robin Turgis he leaves the right he has, as a born Parisian, to be elected *echevin* (in fact, only very wealthy and influential men were elected to that office, although in theory every born Parisian was eligible). He adds that if he now also speaks the dialect of Poitou, it is because two pretty girls taught him.

"They were very pretty and sweet. They live in Saint Generou near Saint Julien de Voventes, on the border of Brittany and Poitou," and, he continues in Poitevin, "But I won't tell you exactly where they can be found every day. Gosh, I'm not that crazy! I want to keep my loves secret."

He remembers the abbess of Port-Royal, his gay companion at many feasts on stolen victuals. This abbess, Huguette du Hamel, was really notorious for her scandalous conduct. When she was finally deposed by the Church, she absconded with her lover, taking the convent treasury with her.

Many others receive ridiculous gifts, until he comes to maître Jean Cotard, his lawyer in ecclesiastical court. This man has recently died, and so he rates this magnificent *ballade*:

> Pere Noé, qui plantastes la vigne
> Vous aussi, Loth, qui bustes au rochier,
> Par tel party qu'Amours, qui gens engigne,
> De vos filles si vous feist approuchier
> (Pas ne le dy pour le vous reprouchier),
> Archetriclin, qui bien sceustes cet art,
> Tous trois vous pry qu'o vous vueillez perchier
> L'ame du bon feu maître Jehan Cotart.
>
> Jadis extraict il fut de vostre ligne,
> Luy qui beuvoit du meilleur et plus chier,
> Et ne deust il avoir vaillant un pigne;
> Certes, sur tous, c'estoit ung bon archier;
> On ne luy sceut pot des mains arrachier;
> De bien boire oncques ne fut fetart.

Nobles seigneurs, ne souffrez empeschier
L'ame du bon feu maistre Jehan Cotart!

Comme homme beu qui chancelle et trepigne
L'ay veu souvent, quant il s'alloit couchier,
Et une fois il se feist une bigne,
Bien m'en souvient, a l'estal d'ung bouchier.
Brief, on n'eust sceu en ce monde serchier
Meilleur pyon, pour boire tost ou tart.
Faictes entrer quant vous orrez huchier
L'ame du bon feu maistre Jehan Cotart.

Prince, il n'eust sceu jusqu'a terre crachier;
Tousjours crioit: "Haro! la gorge m'art."
Et si ne sceut oncq sa seuf estanchier
L'ame du bon feu maistre Jehan Cotart.

(Father Noah, you who planted the vine, you too, Loth, who drank near the rocks in such a manner that Love, which fools people, caused you to approach your daughters in such a way [I do not say this to blame you], Architriclinus, who were well versed in this art—all three of you I pray that you will accept in your midst the soul of the late good master Jean Cotart.

He certainly once came from your lineage, he who drank of the best and most expensive, even when he did not have anything worth a comb on him. Above all, he was a good marksman [= guzzler]; one could not have pried a full tankard out of his hands. He never was lazy when it came to drinking well. Noble Lords, don't let anybody keep out the soul of the late good master Jean Cotart.

I have seen him often as a drunk man who staggers and sways, when he was on his way home, and once he got a huge bump, I remember well, hitting his head against a butcher's sign. In short, one could not have found in this world a better guzzler for drinking early and late. Say, "Please come in," when you hear knock the soul of the late good master Jean Cotart.

Prince, he could not have spat as far as the ground. Always he shouted, "Help! my throat is on fire"! And never was able to quench his thirst the soul of the late good master Jean Cotart.)

The three biblical characters, and therefore saints, who

in their lifetime knew something about drinking, are asked to intercede for this departed arch drinker. Architriclinus, the word which, in the Gospel of John, refers to the chief steward of the bridegroom's house in Cana, was mistaken for the bridegroom's name. Because he was the first to taste the wine which Jesus had made out of water, he is here addressed as a patron saint of wine drinkers. Few drunkards have been awarded such a monument as Cotart was given in this *ballade*.

One bequest follows the other until Villon gives a police clerk a basket full of cloves that the latter will first have to steal. In gratitude for this gift, the police clerk should loyally serve his master, "the knight who serves Saint Christopher." The reference here is to Robert d'Estouteville, Villon's understanding protector, the husband of Ambroise de Loré who is herself fond of poetry. Sir Robert had won this wonderful wife as a prize at a tournament which King René of Anjou-Naples had held in Saumur. The *ballade* which Villon once composed for Robert d'Estouteville is probably one of his earliest. It is very conventional in style and content. It is supposed to express the lucky husband's feelings for his wife. The first two stanzas show her name in acrostic. The refrain is: "Et c'est la fin pour quoy sommes ensemble" ("And this is the reason why we are together").

But now Villon remembers someone "who recommended me so well in Bourges," in other words, slandered him, and so he looks up a famous cookbook to find out how envious tongues should be fried. The recipe he then gives in form of a *ballade* is a challenge to any person's imagination. It would be impossible to invent a longer list of more disgusting things than the ones listed.

A century earlier, Philippe de Vitry, poet and composer, had written in verse one of the first "return to nature" books. It was in praise of the simple life of a couple, Franc Gontier and his wife, who made the best of their poverty and lived most happily on practically nothing. This was not at all

Villon's idea of happiness. Now he sends his refutation of
Franc Gontier and his way of life to a very rich and influential man who had never helped him.

Through a hole in the wall I once saw a fat canon seated on
a soft cushion in a well-matted room, with lady Sidoine lying at
his side, white, tender, smooth, and well attired, drinking hippocras day and night, laughing, kissing, caressing, playing, and,
later, both naked to put their bodies at greater ease. Then I
realized that to appease one's sorrows there is no greater treasure
than to live in comfort.

If Franc Gontier and his wife Helen had ever lived such a
sweet life, they would not have given a toasted t–d for garlic
and onions, which cause bad breath, nor for their curds and all
their stew. I do not say this to blame them. If they brag about
sleeping under the rose bush—which is better, a bed with a chair
next to it? What do you say? Is there any need to muse about
it? There is no greater treasure than to live in comfort.

They live on coarse, dark bread, on barley, on oats, and drink
water all year long. All the birds from here to Babylon could
not hold me for a single day, or even a morning, to such a fare.
Let Franc Gontier have fun, by God, with Helen near him under
the wild rose tree. If they like it, I have no cause to worry. But
whatever may be said about the Life of Work, there is no
greater treasure than to live in comfort.

Prince, be the judge to put a quick end to our dispute. As
for me—but let no one take offense—I have heard it said, when
I was small child: There is no greater treasure than to live in
comfort.

The lady from whose property the famous stone was stolen
by the students, Mademoiselle de Bruyères, was some sort
of self-appointed missionary bent on saving girls from a life
of shame, preaching to them from the Bible. Since the cemetery in crowded Paris was about the only open space, this is
where she gathered the girls around her. Villon intimates
that the sharp-witted and sharp-tongued Parisian girls merely
took advantage of her zeal without heeding her preachings.

The poet suggests that instead of assembling in the cemetery, they should go to the linen market, where incessant
feminine chattering is in place. Yet he likes the chattering
of the Parisian girls, as the next *ballade* says, the one whose
refrain is: "Il n'est bon bec que de Paris."

This refrain is difficult to translate. *Bec* is a bird's bill. As
a metaphor for "the mouth," the word therefore suggests that
the lips are pushed forward, in other words, pursed for kissing. So the sense of the line is: "Only Parisian women can
talk (and kiss) properly."

Otherwise, the *ballade* is again an enumeration, this time
of geographical terms, countries and cities, where the women
are reputed to be great talkers. At one point Villon interrupts himself with the question: "Haven't I mentioned many
places?" Somehow the long list is in no way tedious; the light
tone and the humor keep it amusing throughout. He concludes: "Prince, give the prize for good talking to the women
of Paris, for whatever may be said about Italian girls, *il n'est
bon bec que de Paris.*"

He goes on with a colorful description of the many ways
Parisian girls go about it, and so he finally comes to La
Grosse Margot (Fat Margot).

In his essay on Villon, Gaston Paris deplores the fact that
the *ballade* about La Grosse Margot is so well known and so
famous.[8] He thinks it gives a wrong impression of Villon.
Now, while it is true that this *ballade* is just about the most
ribald poem he ever wrote, there must be a reason for its
popularity. This writer does not believe that one likes it only
for the reason that some people like dirty jokes; there is more
to it than merely reveling in sordid things. Can one perhaps
feel the consciousness of degradation pierce through the tight
cover of this shameless and unmerciful description of an
abominable way of life?

Some critics have even contested that it is Villon himself
who speaks in the first person here. Like the *ballade* for
Robert d'Estouteville, they say, it is meant to express the

feelings of a friend, a lowly one this time, namely the keeper of the tavern named La Grosse Margot (there was one by that name not far from Notre-Dame) and pimp for the girls who worked there. This argument does not seem very convincing. It is far more likely that Villon lived that kind of life at some time or other and that he tried to deaden his own feeling of disgust by this bravado piece of sordid description. And it is, in its way, a masterpiece.

If I love and serve my pretty one gladly, must you regard me as vile or as a fool for that? She has in her all the good points you could wish for. For the love of her I would take up shield and sword. When customers come, I run to fetch a pot and go to the wine without making much noise. I get them water, cheese, bread, and fruit, and when they pay well I say, "*Bene stat* [that's fine]! Come back here when you are in rut again, here, to this brothel where we do our business."

But then there is a great fight when Margot comes to bed without money. I then can't stand her; my heart hates her to death. I get hold of her clothes and swear that I am going to pawn them. She, arms akimbo, calls me Antichrist, screams, and swears by the death of Jesus that I shall not do it. Then I grab a piece of firewood and put some writing on her nose with it, in this brothel where we do our business.

Then peace is made, and she lets go a big fart, for she is more bloated than a poisonous manure beetle. Laughing, she puts her fist on the top of my head, says "Gogo" to me and hits me on the thigh. Both drunk, we then sleep like logs, and upon awakening, when her belly calls, she climbs on me, not to waste her readiness. Under her I moan; she flattens me down like a board. With her lechery she will entirely destroy me in this brothel where we do our business.

Wind, hail, or frost, my bread is baked. I am a whoremaster; the whore sticks to me. Which of us is better? Each suits the other, one is worth the other, it's a matter of bad rat, bad cat. We love filth, filth sticks to us. We flee from honor and it flees from us, in this brothel where we do our business.

The poet now thinks of other brothels, especially those

of Marion l'Idole and of big Jeanne of Brittany, and he comes to the conclusion that since practically every house in Paris is one, there will soon be no need of distinguishing signs.

To Noel Jolis, who is probably the Noel present at the beating which Villon got on account of Katherine de Vausselles, is given a bunch of willow branches gathered in Villon's garden. Chastisement is very good for the soul, and so let Noel have 240 blows administered by Henry (namely Henri Cousin, the hangman of Paris).

Furthermore I do not know what to give to the Hôtel-Dieu and other hospitals for the poor. Jokes are out of place here, for poor people have enough woes. Everybody sends them scraps. The Mendicant friars have had my goose or at least its bones. To little people, little money.

Furthermore I give to my barber, whose name is Colin Galerne and who is a neighbor of Angelot the herbalist, a large block of ice (taken whence? from the Marne), so that he can hibernate comfortably. Let him press it against his stomach; if he manages to do that all winter, he will not be bothered by next summer's heat.

Furthermore, nothing to the Foundlings, but the lost ones [those whose have gone astray, but there is a double pun here] must be comforted. They will be found again without difficulty on top of Marion l'Idole. I shall read to them a lesson from my school, not a long one. Let them not be stubborn or foolish; let them listen, for it is the last:

Fair children, don't lose the prettiest rose on your hat. My young fellows with sticky fingers, if you go to Montpipeau [euphemism for robbery] or to Rueil [euphemism for crooked gambling], keep your skin. For having fooled around in those two places, Colin de Cayeux, believing that an appeal would do him good, lost his.

It is not a trifling game, one in which one loses the body and perhaps also the soul. If you lose, repentance won't do you any good. One dies of it in shame and disgrace, and he who wins will not get Queen Dido of Carthage for a wife either. A man has to be very foolish and infamous to wager so much for so little.

Let everyone listen to me! It is said, and it is the truth, that a wagonload of wine is drunk entirely, by the fire in winter, in the woods in summer. If you have money, it has not grown on trees. So, hurry up and spend it quickly. Who do you see will be your heir? There is no profit in ill-gotten goods.

This thought is carried further in a *ballade*.

Whether you are a seller of indulgences, or a gambler with loaded dice, or a counterfeiter of coins, so you risk being burned like those perjured traitors who are boiled in oil, or whether you be a thief, robbing and pillaging, where does the profit go? What do you think? All to the taverns and the girls.

If you rime, jest, play cymbals and lutes, like a foolish and shameless mountebank, if you play-act, do magic tricks, play the flute; if in towns and cities you perform farces, comedies, and morality plays; if you win with dice, cards, bowling, this also, just listen, goes all to the taverns and the girls.

If you shrink back from such bad things, then plow, mow fields and meadows, care for and groom horses and mules. If you are totally illiterate, you will have enough, provided you are patient. But if you are one who breaks and combs hemp, be careful that the money you will earn will not all go to the taverns and the girls.

Before you do any worse, carry your shoes, your well-tailored coats, your robes and all your other clothes straight to the taverns and the girls.

A little further on, Villon makes a noteworthy bequest to the Quinze-Vingts, the hospital for the blind. It was called "Quinze-Vingts" (Fifteen Score) because it could accommodate three hundred inmates.

Furthermore, I leave to the Fifteen Score, who might just as well be called the Three Hundred, from Paris, not from Provins, for to them I feel beholden. They shall have, I give my consent, my large spectacles, without the case, so that they

may be able at the Cemetery of the Innocents to distinguish the
skeletons of the honest from those of the dishonest.

The Cemetery of the Innocents! For more than four centuries it had been the only one in Paris. Every few years
the bones had to be dug up to make room for new graves.
These bones were then put into an ossuary, but this, too,
was already crammed to the rafters. So skulls and pelvises
were piled up around it. On the wall above these bones was
painted one of the earliest death dances. According to de-
scriptions by visiting travelers, including Greeks and Italians,
this painting was masterfully executed and most impressive.
It certainly was placed in the right setting.

Who can now tell the great lady from the stable groom? Can
you see by these skulls who was pretty and who was not?

Piled up pellmell on one heap, their feudal estates have been
taken away from them; you cannot call master or clerk.

They are dead; God keep their souls! As for the bodies, they
are rotten, whether they used to be lords and ladies brought up
on sweet, tender food, cream, raisin custard, rice. Their bones
are reduced to powder that does not care anymore for gambols
and laughter. May it please sweet Jesus to absolve them.

For the departed I make this legacy, and this I make known
to regents, courts, tribunals, and palaces of justice, who all hate
iniquitous avarice and who, for the common good, let their
own bones and bodies go dry. May they be absolved by God
and Saint Dominic when they die.

Furthermore, nothing for Jacquet Cardon, for I have nothing
decent to leave him. It isn't that I completely leave him out;
I have for him this *bergeronnette,* that would go to the tune of
"Marionette," once composed for Marion la Peautarde, or to the
tune of "Open Your Door, Guillemette." That girl certainly
went about her business well!

> Au retour de dure prison,
> Ou j'ai laissié presque la vie,
> Se Fortune a sur moy envie.

Jugiez s'elle fait mesprison!
Il me semble que, par raison,
Elle deust bien estre assouvie,
Au retour de dure prison,
Ou j'ai laissié presque la vie.

Se si plaine est de desraison
Que vueille que du tout devie,
Plaise a Dieu que l'ame ravie
En soit lassus en sa maison,
Au retour de dure prison,
Ou j'ai laissié presque la vie.

(After my return from harsh imprisonment, where I almost lost my life, if Fortune is still envious of me, judge how mistaken she must be! It seems to me, in good reason, she ought to be appeased after my return from harsh imprisonment, where I almost lost my life.

If she is so entirely unreasonable that she wishes my total undoing, may it please God that the soul snatched away will dwell up there in its home, after my return from harsh imprisonment, where I almost lost my life.)

Bequest follows bequest, and then come stipulations concerning his burial.

XII *Burial*

Furthermore, I want my grave to be in Sainte Avoie, nowhere else, and so that everybody can see me, not in the flesh, but in a painting, and that the portrait be drawn in ink, if that does not cost too much. A tomb? No, I don't care for one. It would be too heavy for the floor anyhow. [The burial place here mentioned was the chapel of a hospital, located on the second floor.]

Furthermore, I wish that around my pit be written what follows, in large letters, and for lack of other writing materials, in charcoal or with a black stone, but without damaging the plaster. Thus at least I will be remembered as one who liked to have a gay time.)

Ci gist et dort en ce sollier,
Qu'Amours occist de son raillon,
Ung povre petit escollier,
Qui fut nommé Françoys Villon
Oncques de terre n'ot sillon.
Il donna tout, chascun le scet:
Tables, tresteaulx, pain, corbeillon,
Gallans, dictes en ce verset:

Repos eternel donne a cil,
Sire, et clarté perpetuelle,
Qui vaillant plat ni escuelle
N'eut oncques, n'ung brain de percil.
Il fut rez, chief, barbe et sourcil,
Comme ung navet qu'on ret ou pelle.
Repos eternel donne a cil.

Rigueur le transmit en exil,
Et luy frappa au cul la pelle,
Non obstant qu'il dit: "J'en appelle!"
Qui n'est pas terme trop subtil.
Repos eternel donne a cil.

(Here lies and sleeps in this upstairs room he whom Love killed with his arrow, a poor little scholar who was named François Villon. He never owned a single furrow of land. He gave everything, all know it: table, table legs, bread, basket. Young fellows, say this verse about him:

Give this man eternal rest, Lord, and everlasting light, he who never had anything worth a plate or a bowl, or even a sprig of parsley. He was all hairless, head, beard, and brows, like a turnip shaved or peeled. Give this man eternal rest.

Harshness sent him into exile and hit him on the arse with a shovel, although he shouted: "I appeal!"—which was not too subtle a thing to say. Give this man eternal rest.)

All that is left to do now is to name his executors. Of course the poet chooses some very wealthy men who did not know him from Adam. And since one has to pardon everybody before dying, he cries out his pardon to all people in the form of a *ballade*.

To Carthusians and Celestines, to Mendicants and pious sisters, to loafers and double-sole-clappers, to servants and cute girls wearing surcoats and tight-fitting gowns, to love-struck dandies who put on tight tan boots without complaining, to all and sundry I cry out my pardon.

To whores who show their breasts in order to have more customers, to swindlers, starters of brawls, fighters, trainers of marmots, to fools and nitwits of both sexes that go about whistling, six abreast, to little boys and little girls, to all and sundry I cry out my pardon.

But not to those vile sons of bitches who made me s—t hard t—ds and gnash my teeth many an evening and many a morning, though now I no longer fear them the least bit. I would give them farts and belches, but I can't, for I am seated. But anyhow, in order to avoid trouble, to all and sundry I cry out my pardon.

Let their fifteen ribs be crushed with heavy mallets, powerful and massive, with clubs and balls of lead. To all and sundry I cry out my pardon.

Another *ballade* by way of conclusion:

Here is closed and ends the testament of poor Villon. Come to his funeral when you hear the bell, come dressed in the brightest red, for he died a martyr of Love; this he swore upon his testicle when he made ready to leave this world.

I am sure he is not lying about it, for he was heinously chased from his loves like some filthy slob, so much so that from here to Roussillon there is not a single bush or shrub that does not have—he says it truthfully—some shred of his clothing, when he made ready to leave this world.

So it is, and so much so that at time of death he had only one single rag. What's more, as he was dying, Love stabbed him badly with his dart—a thing which, to our astonishment, hurt him worse than the tongue of a belt buckle—when he made ready to leave this world.

Prince as well bred as a hunting falcon, hear what he did before departing: he drank one good gulp of dark red wine when he made ready to leave this world.

And this actually is the end of the "Testament."

CHAPTER 6

Miscellaneous Poems

VILLON had written more poems that he did not care to insert into the "Testament." After finishing this work, and both before his new misfortunes began and during the anxious days when he faced execution, he wrote a few more. Although these poems were scattered around in manuscript form, they were later faithfully collected by students who were proud of their poet. As will invariably happen in such cases, a considerable number of unsigned poems were put into this growing collection. At the time the printing press had come to Paris, therefore, this stack of manuscripts contained many more poems that could not possibly have been written by Villon than genuine pieces. Since the students remembered him primarily as a bold prankster, they attributed to him everything that had to do with such exploits. Those who had known him better or knew him only through his other works soon felt the need to unscramble this motley mass of writing and to separate those poems which were unmistakably his from those merely attributed to him.

The first nearly authoritative printed edition was prepared with great care by Clément Marot (1495-1544).[9] Himself a poet and also a scholar, Marot had a good feeling for Villon's tone, and he was, on the whole, quite successful in identifying the genuine works. In his edition he added a number of the others under the heading, "Poems attributed to Villon," discarding many as surely unauthentic.

Since that time modern scholarship has been at work and has been able to settle more definitely the question as to

what is Villon's and what is not. There are still a few doubtful pieces, and among those discarded there may have been
some of his very early poems which did not yet show his
stamp. Yet, on the whole, the seventeen pieces accepted by
Longnon can be said to well represent the remainder of
Villon's work.

I Ballade *of Sound Advice*

The first on this list is a *ballade* largely based on St.
Paul's Epistle to the Romans. It is a bit flat, evidently an
early work. We recognize the Villon we know in a few
passages only and in the fact that the chief warning, which
is repeated in the refrain, cautions the reader against stealing.

II *Proverbs*

Next comes a *ballade* on proverbs. It was probably an
accomplishment to collect thirty-two samples of this homely
wisdom, all beginning with *tant* (so much), and to arrange
them according to the rime-scheme of a *ballade*. This, aside
from the earthy message of the proverbs themselves, con-
stitutes its only merit.

III *Small Talk*

Not much better is the "Ballade des Menus Propos," the
small talk *ballade*, although its refrain echoes Socrates'
primary injunction: "Je congnois tout, fors que moy mesmes"
("I know everything except myself"). It is indeed small
talk, and every line begins with the words: "Je congnois."

IV *Counter-truths*

A well established method in teaching moral principles
was to make a list of counter-truths. The pedagogical reason-

ing behind this surprising technique was that the reader or listener, faced with an evidently untrue statement, would respond by actively constructing the true statement, which would then imprint itself into his conscience more firmly than would a mere preaching. In this poem, therefore, there are twenty-six statements calculated to shock the reader into finding the truth. The refrain says, "No one is well advised except a man in love."

V *Against the Enemies of France*

There is some doubt as to Villon's authorship in the case of the next poem. If written by him, and it well may be, it would be the other tiny piece of evidence for his having been a great patriot (the other one being his including Joan of Arc among the departed ladies). This poem presents a long list of horrible punishments for anyone "qui mal vouldroit au royaulme de France" ("who would wish evil on the kingdom of France").

The poem is full of mythology and biblical history. Jason and Nebuchadnezzar, Tantalus and Mary Magdalen, Jonah, Job, Jupiter, and Venus, Absalom and Sardanapalus, who all suffered or inflicted punishments that would be fitting for the enemies of France.

There follows a little *rondeau* by Villon or someone else. The word "cute" seems to be in place here.

Jenin l'Avenu
Va-t-en aux estuves;
Et toy la venu,
Jenin l'Avenu,
Si te lave nud
Et te baigne es cuves.
Jenin l'Avenu,
Va-t-en aux estuves.

(Jenin l'Avenu, go take a bath, and once you are there, Jenin l'Avenu, wash yourself naked and bathe in the tub. Jenin l'Avenu, go take a bath.)

VI *The Ballad of Blois*

If Villon's authorship is contested in the case of this insignificant ditty—it has to be read aloud in French to reveal its charm—the next poem is surely by him, and on the authority of the trustworthy Duke of Orléans. I have already discussed this poem and the circumstances of its origin. It was a contest; the theme was given in the line, "Je meurs de seuf auprès de la fontaine" ("I am dying of thirst next to the fountain"), and every line was to contain a contradiction. The refrain was to be: "Bien receully, debouté de chascun" ("Well received, pushed away by everyone").

Considering these severe limitations in addition to the strict demands of the *ballade* form, this poem is a masterpiece of poetic technique and well deserved being included in Duke Charles's collection.

VII *Poems to Marie d'Orléans*

The same duke is indirectly addressed in the next poem, but here we are completely in the dark as to the circumstances. The birth of a daughter in 1457 was indeed a happy event, for the couple had been childless until then, and the duchess was close to the years when no children could be expected. There was great rejoicing, also, in the good town of Orléans, when the little princess made her entry some two years later. But what did this all mean to Villon? He praises her or her most fortuitous birth in a total of three poems. The first, which is called a *Dit* (statement), has no particularly elaborate form; on the other hand, it has a style so panegyrical that the meaning is hard to see through the clouds of incense.

The second poem of this series, which is a *double ballade,* offers a clue that does not help much. One of the stanzas reads:

> Cy, devant Dieu, fais congnoissance
> Que creature feusse morte,
> Ne feust vostre doulce naissance,
> En charité puissant et forte,
> Qui ressuscite et reconforte
> Ce que Mort avoit prins pour sien.
> Vostre presence me conforte:
> On doit dire du bien le bien.

(Here, before God, I testify that I would be a a dead creature if it had not been for your sweet birth, so powerful and strong in charity, which brings back to life and comforts that which Death had already considered his. Your presence consoles me: about the good one must say the good.)

Did her birth really save Villon from death? Some think so. But considering the manner in which he thanked the king for his fortuitous passage through Meung, it is logical to assume that if he had been saved from the gallows by the happy event, he would have expressed in less tortuous terms what he thanked the little girl for. Perhaps it was then that Charles d'Orléans, congratulated in some lost poem, decided to attach Villon to his court. In that case, the death mentioned above would be a figure of speech.

The entire series of the poems addressed to Marie d'Orléans is prefaced by a quotation from Virgil, from that Eclogue which was regarded as a prophecy of the birth of Christ: "Jam nova progenies caelo demittitur alto" ("already a new progeny is sent down from heaven"). The third poem of the series takes up these lines again and paraphrases them. The last two stanzas read:

> Dont resume ce que j'ay dit:
> "Nova progenies celo"
> Car c'est du poëte le dit,
> "Jamjam demittitur alto."

Saige Cassandre, belle Echo,
Digne Judith, caste Lucresse,
Je vous congnois, noble Dido,
A ma seule dame et maistresse.

En priant Dieu, digne pucelle,
Qu'il vous doint longue et bonne vie;
Qui vous ayme, ma damoiselle,
Ja ne coure sur luy envie.
Entiere dame et assouvie,
J'espoir de vous servir ainçoys,
Certes, se Dieu plaist, que devie
Vostre povre escolier Françoys.

(So I resume what I have said: "Already a new progeny." This
is what the poet said, "is sent down from the high heavens."
Wise Cassandra, beautiful Echo, worthy Judith, chaste Lucrece,
I recognize you, noble Dido, as my only lady and mistress.

Praying to God, worthy maiden, that He give you a long and
good life. May he who loves you never be attacked by envy.
You, accomplished lady, I hope to serve you some time, certainly,
if it please God to keep me alive, your poor scholar François.)

It is good to remember that these words were addressed
to a baby, either newly born or, at the most, two years old.
The style of these three poems seems to support the assumption that Villon's encounter with the little girl's father
took place before the terrible experience of the imprisonment in Meung. It is the style of the fictitious love complaints in the "Legacy," plus a deliberate attempt to be as
"courtly" as possible. The poet had not yet entirely found
himself. The "high" style was never his forte, either in the
ballade for Robert d'Estouteville or, much later, in his poem
of thanks to the Parlement of Paris.

VIII   *To the Duke of Bourbon*

Villon is easily recognizable again, however, in his "Re-
queste à Monseigneur de Bourbon."

My Lord and recognized prince, bloom of the lily, royal off-spring, François Villon, whom Hardship has tamed with blunt blows and awful beatings, begs you in this humble writing to grant him graciously some little loan. He is ready to sign his obligation in all the courts, and so surely you will not doubt that he will satisfy you: you will suffer no loss, but get no interest either. All you will lose will be the time spent waiting.

Your humble creature has never borrowed a penny from any prince except you; you loaned him six *écus*; these he has gradually converted into food. All will be repaid together, as is proper, and it will be done lightly and quickly, for as soon as I find acorns in the forest around Patay [where there are no oaks] and chestnuts are being sold, you will be repaid without delay or stopping. All you will lose will be the time spent waiting.

If I could sell a part of my health to a Lombard (they are all usurers by nature), the lack of money has so completely over-powered me that I would take that chance, I believe. I do not hang any money on my coat or my belt. Good Lord! I am amazed that no cross ever appears before me [coins had a cross on their reverse side], except one of wood or stone; I am not lying. But if once at least the true cross would appear before me, all you would lose would be the time spent waiting.

Prince of the lily, you who take pleasure in everything good, have you ever thought how much I hate never to come up to my intentions? You understand, help me please. All you will lose will be the time spent waiting.

The joke about the true cross, meaning here, of course, the one on the back of coins, borders on blasphemy, but, in general, people were not very sensitive about that.

Underneath the letter are written these four send-off lines:

> Allez, lettres, faictes ung sault;
> Combien que n'ayez pié ne langue,
> Remonstrez en vostre harangue
> Que faulte d'argent si m'assault.

(Go, letter, take a leap; although you have neither foot nor tongue, explain in your harangue that it is lack of money that so assails me.)

We do not know if the duke responded. He very probably did. But if he did, it certainly was with no loan.

IX *Outcry from Prison*

In view of Villon's terrible imprisonment in the dungeon of Meung, no one certainly would expect him to have written a *ballade* there. Even if he had been able somehow to obtain writing materials, he could not have hoped that the message would ever reach his friends. Yet this is what the next poem purports to be: an appeal to his friends, written in the prison of Meung. It is easily conceivable however, that he composed the *ballade* there in the depth of the dungeon and that he recited it aloud to the damp walls. It would have helped his spirits to assert himself as a poet while deprived of everything, even the free use of his hands. This is a more satisfactory assumption than that the poem was composed only when it could be written down, namely, after his release, and that it is, at best, a flashback, a reminiscence. His reminiscences of Meung, we have already seen, are of a different nature. The crude third stanza of the *ballade* in which he pardons everybody or his "prayers" for Thibaut d'Aussigny are good examples of his violent feelings on that matter. I do not believe that Villon would have written a *ballade* like the following after his release. A mood we frequently find in him is bravado, so that, by composing this *ballade* orally in the darkness of his prison and shouting it at the walls, he would have defied the bishop and his henchmen. The poem is not an outcry of despair; it resembles in no way a *de profundis*. He has no illusion about his friends hearing him. His friends go on with their frivolous pursuits while he rots away. Of course, they will leave him there. He is enough of a cynic to know that. The refrain, "Le lesserez la, le povre Villon?" is a rhetorical question. It is, incidentally, another one of the refrains that stand out rhythmically: it is most unusual to divide a ten-syllable verse exactly in the middle: "Will you leave him there, the wretched Villon?"

If the first line still sounds like a desperate appeal, irony immediately takes over in the following lines. The indirectness thus achieved makes the poem all the more pathetic.

> Aiez pitié, aiez pitié de moy,
> A tout le moins, si vous plaist, mes amis!
> En fosse gis, non pas soubs houx ne may,
> En cest exil ouquel je suis transmis
> Par Fortune, comme Dieu l'a permis.
> Filles, amans, jeunes gens et nouveaulx,
> Danceurs, saulteurs, faisans les piez de veaux,
> Vifs comme dars, agus comme aguillon,
> Gousiers tintans cler comme cascaveaux
> Le lesserez la, le povre Villon?
>
> Chantres chantans a plaisance, sans loy
> Galans, rians, plaisans en fais et dis,
> Courens, alans, francs de faulx or, d'aloy,
> Gens d'esperit, ung petit estourdis,
> Trop demourez, car il meurt entandis,
> Faiseurs de laiz, de motetz et rondeaux,
> Quant mort sera, vous luy ferez chaudeaulx!
> Ou gist, il n'entre escler ne tourbillon:
> De murs espoix on lui a fait bandeaux.
> Le lesserez la, le povre Villon?
>
> Venez le veoir en ce piteux arroy,
> Nobles hommes, francs de quart et de dix,
> Qui ne tenez d'empereur ne de roy,
> Mais seulement de Dieu de Paradis:
> Jeuner lui fault dimenches et merdis,
> Dont les dens a plus longues que ratteaux;
> Après pain sec, non pas après gasteaux,
> En ses boyaulx verse eaue a gros bouillon;
> Bas en terre, table n'a ne tresteaulx.
> Le lesserez la, le povre Villon?
>
> Princes nommez, ancïens, jouvenceaux,
> Impetrez moy graces et royaulx seaux,

Et me montez en quelque corbillon.
Ansi le font, l'un a l'autre, pourceaux,
Car ou l'un brait, ils fuyent a monceaux.
Le lesserez la, le povre Villon?

(Pity, pity me, at least you, if you please, my friends! I lie in a pit, not under holly or green branches, in this exile where I was placed by Fortune, as God permitted. Girls, lovers, youths and boys, dancers, jumpers, doing the calf-foot step, lively as darts, sharp as stings, throats ringing clear as bells, will you leave him there, the wretched Villon?

Singers singing as you please, without rules, laughing gallants pleasing in what they do and say, running, going, free from false gold, from alloy, men of wit, a little bit scatterbrained, you are waiting too long, for he is dying in the meanwhile. Makers of lais, of motets and rondeaux, when he is dead, you will make rich soups for him! Where he lies neither lightning nor whirlstorm can enter: with thick walls they have bandaged his eyes. Will you leave him there, the wretched Villon?

Come to see him in this pitiful array, you noblemen who are free from taxes and tithes, who hold no land from emperor or king but only from God in heaven. He has to fast on Tuesdays and Sundays from which his teeth have become longer than those of a rake; after dry bread, not after cake, he pours water into his bowels in large streams; low in the ground, he has no table or trestles [table legs]. Will you leave him there, the wretched Villon?

Princes named, old and young, get for me letters of grace and royal seals, and pull me up in a basket. This is the way pigs act one toward the other, for as soon as one squeals, they all come running in a heap. Will you leave him there, the wretched Villon?)

Fasting on Sundays and Tuesdays means fasting all week, for to the rigorous ascetic all the other days were fast days. The water poured into his bowels may be an allusion to the terrible water torture. And Villon expects his friends to be as decent as pigs!

X *Debate between Heart and Body*

Ever since the twelfth century, poets liked to express psychological musings in the form of a debate between the heart and the body. There is an infinity of such debates, some naïve, some philosophical, but all based on extremely primitive and undifferentiated notions of psychology. Many are quite abstract, impersonal, little more than an excuse to display scholarship, biblical or philosophical; others refer to a definite problem, mostly love. Even on that topic there can be no infinite variety: the heart will reproach the body for being too slow in the service of the lady, or it will reproach it for falling in love at all.

It is not difficult to see why Villon should have chosen this time-honored form, and it could likewise be expected that in his case the debate would be neither abstract nor impersonal. The heart, the inner voice, had only too much disquieting reality for him. The traditional form of a written dialogue is nothing but the expression of that secret dialogue we always hold within ourselves when we take stock of who we are and where we stand.

This dialogue is hard to translate or paraphrase. I therefore give it here in Bonner's excellent translation.

"What do I hear?"—"It's me."—"Who?"—"Your heart
which hangs on only by a tender thread.
My strength ebbs, my vital sap is drained
when I see you so withdrawn and lonely
like some poor dog crouching in a corner.
And why is that? Because you lead a madcap life."—
"What difference does it make?"—"I get the worst of it."—
"Leave me alone! Why, you ask? I'll think about it."—
"When will that be?"—"When my childhood's over."—
"I say no more."—"That's quite alright with me."

"What's your intent?"—"To be a man of merit."—
"You're thirty years of age."—"Just like a mule."—

"Is that still childhood?"—"No."—"Then madness
has got hold of you."—"Hold of what? My collar?"—
"You don't know a thing."—"Yes I do: flies in milk.
The difference is that one is black and one is white."—
"Is that all?"—"You still want me to argue?
If that is not enough I'll start again."—
"You're lost!"—"I'll try to straighten out."—
"I say no more."—"That's quite alright with me."

"From this I get the sorrow, you the harm and pain.
If you had been some poor mad fool, then
I might have had some reason for excusing you;
But you don't care: good and bad are all the same to you.
It's either that your head is hard as rock,
or else you like misfortune more than honor.
What can you answer to this argument?"—
"I'll be above it when I pass away."—"God, what
consolation!"—"What wisdom and what eloquence!"—
"I say no more."—"That's quite alright with me."

"Whence come these ills?"—"They come from my bad luck.
When Saturn packed my bag for me,
he put them in, I think."—"That's foolishness.
You are his lord and feel yourself his servant.
Look what Solomon has written in his scroll:
'A wise man,' he says, 'has power
over planets and their influence.' "—
"I don't believe it; as they have made me, thus I'll be."—
"What did you say?"—"Yes, this is my belief."—
"I say no more."—"That's quite alright with me."

"You want to live?"—"God give me strength to do so!"—
"You then must . . . ."—"What?"—"Feel penitent and read
unceasingly."—"What sort of thing?"—"Graver subjects,
and leave your foolish friends."—"I'll think about it."—
"Now don't forget."—"I've made a note of it."—
"Don't wait so long that things get worse.
I say no more."—"That's quite alright with me." (B)

XI   Ballade *on Fortune*

Could Villon go on blaming his bad luck for all his misfortunes? Had the planets been against him? Had he been
dealt such a bad hand of cards that he could not possibly
win? In the dungeon and after his release, he had given
much thought to this problem—the problem of Fortune. This
is the title he gave his *ballade* when he seemed to hear
Dame Fortune herself answer his anxious question and, in
so doing, justify his own inability to withstand her.

I was named Fortune by the scholars of the past, I whom you,
François, decry and call a murderess, you who are a man without any fame at all. I have made better men than you make
plaster or dig stones in a quarry. If you live shamefully, must
you complain? You are not alone; you should not feel sorry for
yourself. Look and see some of my former deeds, many fine men
dead and stiff by my doing. Compared to them, you know it,
you are only a slob. Relax, and stop talking. On my advice, take
everything in your stride, Villon.

Against great kings I stirred quite powerfully in olden days.
I killed Priam and his whole army; tower, dungeon, and forti-
fications were of no use to him. And did Hannibal stay behind?
I struck at him with death in Carthage. I snuffed out Scipio
the African and sold Julius Caesar to the senate. In Egypt I
destroyed Pompey, and I drowned Jason in a whirlpool in the
sea. One time I even burned Rome and the Romans. On my
advice, take everything in your stride, Villon.

Alexander who fought so many battles, who wanted to see
the Polar star—his body was poisoned by me. King Alphasar
was dragged to death in a field on his flag. That is the way I do
things. So I did, and so I shall continue; I will not give any
other cause or reason for it. Holophernes, the accursed idolater,
was slain with his own weapon by Judith while he was asleep
inside his tent. Absalom, what of him? As he fled, I hanged him.
On my advice, take everything in your stride, Villon.

Therefore, François, listen to what I say: If I could act without
being checked by God in heaven, I would not leave you one

single rag, neither you nor anyone else; instead of one ill, I would
deliver ten. On my advice, take everything in your stride, Villon.

XII   *Facing Execution*

But can a man take it in his stride when he has been sentenced to death and it is more than probable that he will be
executed? The fact is that it was doubtful that the appeal
to Parlement would be heeded. Villon's customary bravado
exhausted itself in the four lines:

> Je suis Françoys, dont il me poise,
> Né de Paris, emprès Pontoise,
> Et de la corde d'une toise
> Sçaura mon col que mon cul poise.

(I am François, sorry to say, born in Paris, near Pontoise, and
at the end of a rope one toise long my neck will know the weight
of my arse.)

Here the execution is faced as a certainty, but then the
horrible vision of corpses dangling from the gallows haunted
him too much. He wrote the *ballade* which alone would grant
him immortality.

> Freres humains qui apres nous vivez,
> n'ayez les cuers contre nous endurcis,
> Car, se pitié de nous povres avez,
> Dieu en aura plus tost de vous mercis.
> Vous nous voiez cy attachez cinq, six:
> Quant de la chair, que trop avons nourrie,
> Elle est pieça devorée et pourrie,
> Et nous, les os, devenons cendre et pouldre.
> De notre mal personne ne s'en rie;
> Mais priez Dieu que tous nous vueil absouldre!
>
> Se vous clamons freres, pas n'en devez
> Avoir desdaing, quoy que fusmes occis

Par justice. Toutesfois, vous sçavez
Que tous hommes n'ont pas bon sens rassis;
Excusez nous puis que sommes transsis,
Envers le fils de la Vierge Marie,
Que sa grace ne soit pour nous tarie,
Nous preservant de l'infernale fouldre.
Nous sommes mors, ame ne nous harie;
Mais priez Dieu que tous nous vueil absouldre.

La pluye nous a debuez et lavez,
Et le soleil dessechiez et noircis;
Pies, corbeaulx, nous ont les yeux cavez,
Et arrachié la barbe et les sourcis.
Jamais nul temps nous ne sommes assis;
Puis ça, puis la, comment le vent varie,
A son plaisir sans cesser nous charie,
Plus becquetez d'oiseaulx que dez a couldre.
Ne soyez pas de notre confrairie:
Mais priez Dieu que tous nous vueil absouldre!

Prince Jhesus, qui sur nous a maistrie,
Garde qu'Enfer n'ait de nous seigneurie:
A luy n'ayons que faire ne que souldre.
Hommes, icy n'a point de mocquerie,
Mais priez Dieu que tous nous vueil absouldre!

(Human brothers who live on after us, don't let your hearts be hardened against us, for if you have pity for us poor men, God will more readily have pity for you. You see us here, strung up, five, six of us. As for the flesh, which we had fed too well, it has long since been eaten and has rotted, and we, the bones, are turning into ashes and dust. Let no one laugh at our misfortune, but pray to God that He may absolve us all!

If we call you brothers, you must not despise us because we were killed by justice. After all, you know that not all men have good sound sense. Commend us, since we have passed away, to the Son of the Virgin Mary, that His grace will not dry up for us, but will preserve us from the thunderbolt of hell. We are dead, let no soul harass us, but pray to God that He may absolve us all.

Rain has laundered and washed us, and the sun has dried and blackened us. Magpies, crows, have hollowed out our eyes and torn off beard and brows. At no time are we ever at rest: now back, now forth; as the wind changes, it pushes us around incessantly at its pleasure; birds' bills have bored more holes into us than are in thimbles. Do not join our brotherhood, but pray to God that He may absolve us all!

Prince Jesus, who has power over all, see to it that Hell will not get us into its power, that we have nothing to do or to solve there. Men, here there is no room for scornful laughter, but pray to God that He may absolve us all!)

The vision remained deeply imprinted with all its horrors, but the certainty of death was suddenly taken away. To be sure, Villon would have to leave Paris, and that was a punishment of great severity; but at least he would not be hanged. But he needed a little time to say goodbye to friends and to put his affairs in order. So, in a poem addressed to the Parlement, the high court of Paris, Villon combined his thanks for the reprieve with a request for three days of grace. It is one of his worst poems, another complete failure in an attempt to use an elevated style. He is following a pattern, but he follows it badly. His praise of the court is so bombastic that the refrain, "Mother of the good and Sister of the blessed angels," is not even the poorest line.

XIII *Praise of Parlement*

Villon summons his five senses—for the tongue alone would not be enough!—to express his grateful respect to the sovereign court. The fact that the word "court" is feminine in French justifies the use of the words "Mother" and "Sister" in the refrain.

In the second stanza he summons his heart to burst open, not to be as hard as the rock from which Moses drew water, and to join in with all his tears in the praise of the court.

In the third stanza, however, a little bit of the true Villon

shines through the bombast: he begs his teeth to come out,
one by one, since they will never have to worry about having anything to chew, and to sing a chorus of praise louder
than organ, trumpet, and bell: "and you, my body, who are
vile and worse than bear or hog that make their nest in their
own dirt, praise the court."

In the *envoi*, too, he is laudably direct:

Prince, please grant me three days, so that I can prepare myself
and say goodbye to friends and folks. Without them I have no
money, neither on me nor at the changers' bank. Triumphant
court, let it be, do not deny it me, Mother of the good and Sister
of the blessed angels.

XIV *Farewell to the Jailer*

It is good that the poem of thanks and praise to the Parlement is not our last impression of Villon. It is followed by
a *ballade* addressed to the turnkey of the Châtelet, a man
he knew quite well and who had joined the police in order
not to be overpowered by them, as many others did. Etienne
Garnier would understand that Villon had been released by
order of the high court on the basis of an appeal and not
because he had turned informer on the Coquille. Surely
Garnier still had connections with that brotherhood and
could let them know what had happened.

> Que vous semble de mon appel,
> Garnier? Feis je sens ou folie?
> Toute beste garde sa pel;
> Qui la contraint, efforce ou lie,
> S'elle peult, elle se deslie.
> Quant donc par plaisir voluntaire
> Chantée me fut ceste omelie,
> Estoit il lors temps de moy taire?
>
> Se feusse des hoirs Hue Cappel,
> Qui fut extrait de boucherie,

On ne m'eust, parmy ce drappel,
Fait boire en ceste escorcherie.
Vous entendez bien joncherie?
Mais quant ceste paine arbitraire
On me jugea par tricherie,
Estoit il lors temps de moy taire?

Cuidiez vous que soubs mon cappel
N'y eust tant de philosophie
Comment de dire: "J'en appel"?
Si avoit, je vous certiffie,
Combien que point trop ne m'y fie.
Quant on me dist, present notaire:
"Pendu serez!" je vous affie,
Estoit il lors temps de moy taire?

Prince, se j'eusse eu la pepie,
Pieça je feusse ou est Clotaire,
Aux champs debout comme une espie.
Estoit il lors temps de moy taire?

(What do you think of my appeal, Garnier? Did I do the right thing or was I foolish? Every beast tries to keep his skin. If he gets confined, overpowered, bound, he will escape, if he can. So when, by sheer arbitrary pleasure, that homily was sung to me, was it then time to keep my mouth shut?

If I were an heir of Hugh Capet, who was the descendant of a butcher, they would not have made me drink that torment through a rag. You understand my joke? But when they sentenced me by trickery to that arbitrary punishment, was it then time to keep my mouth shut?

Did you really think I did not have that much philosophy under my cap, enough to say, "I appeal!" I did have it, I assure you, although I did not have too much confidence in it when, in presence of a notary, they told me, "You will be hanged!" Was it then time to keep my mouth shut?

Prince, if I had had laryngitis, I would long since be where Clotaire is, or hoisted up outdoors like a spy. Was it then time to keep my mouth shut?)

Here the reference to the water torture is not an exaggeration as it may be in the poem from Meung. It is explicitly stated that he was subjected to that torment, and the Parlement agrees with Villon that there was no cause to treat him that badly. What the trickery was on the basis of which they pronounced the death sentence is not known; it was possibly a confession made under torture, but not confirmed later. Clotaire was the name of several Merovingian kings; to be where they were, consequently, meant to be dead.

This poem, which reveals once more Villon's bravado, is the last he is known to have composed.

CHAPTER 7

Poems in Jargon

THE poems which Villon wrote in the secret language of the Coquille have always fascinated linguists, literary scholars, and fellow poets. There is, first, the challenge of their incomprehensibility. In spite of all research, only a few words of the Coquille slang have been identified, and of these only a few occur in Villon's poems. Some can be guessed with a fair degree of certainty, others have been rendered differently by every would-be translator. On the other hand, these poems read magnificently if one is not concerned with the exact meaning. They are as perfect in form as Villon's French *ballades* and *rondeaux*. One, in particular, has always struck this writer as an ideal marching song. It has the rimes of a *ballade* through three stanzas and an *envoi*, but the meter is quite unusual. I give here the first stanza to convey an idea of the form.

> Spelicans
>   Qui en tous temps
> Avancez dedans le pogois
>   Gourde piarde
>   Et sur la tarde
> Desbousez les povres nyais,
> Et pour soustenir vos pois
>   Sans faire haire
>   Ne hault braire,
> Mais plantez ils sont comme joncs
> Par les sires qui sont si longs.

The reader must not be dismayed if he cannot understand these lines. All attempts to translate this magnificent poem are pure guesswork. Surely there is something sinister about "les sires qui sont si longs," the sires that are so long, and scholars have found that "pogois" means money. Normally, when people devise a "secret" language, the nouns and adjectives are invented, whereas the verbs and the little words remain the same. Above all, the syntax is unaffected, and the general sound is retained. The quoted stanza is unmistakably French, although no Frenchman can understand it.

Until recently only six of these jargon *ballades* were known. Then a seventh was found in a Stockholm manuscript that could readily be ascribed to Villon since his name appears in acrostic in the *envoi*. It is not, however, a perfect acrostic.

> Vive David! saint archquin la baboue
> Iehan mon amy, qui les fueilles desnoue.
> Le vendengeur, beffleur comme une choue,
> Loing de son plain, de ses flos curieulx,
> Noe beaucoup, dont il reçoit fressoue,
> Jonc verdoiant, havre du marieux.

It is impossible to say more about these poems. In only the most general sense can the meaning be guessed. It is generally assumed that all these poems were written during the long period of Villon's involuntary wandering that ultimately led to the prison in Meung.

CHAPTER 8

Assessment

THE many images of Villon have now condensed into one discernible personality, one, indeed, with many facets, but consistent and clearly delineated. Some of the images still frequently encountered have vanished from sight. Gone is the nature poet who "sang as the birds sing": birds do not sing in such perfectly mastered and rigidly controlled form. Gone also is the carefree vagabond, for whenever he was forced by unfortunate circumstances to be a vagabond, he certainly was not carefree. A tavern minstrel he may have been in his student days, but only in the sense that he read or recited his poems to groups of appreciative students assembled in a tavern. A criminal he was, but not a hardened one, for, in spite of all bravado, the gallows frightened him and he could never entirely shut his inner ear to the voice of his "heart." He never lost his feeling for his mother and his deep understanding of her plain, untutored piety, nor his gratitude to maître Guillaume Villon, his "more than father," whose name he made famous.

Certainly, Villon was no beatnik, hippie, or digger, and he was a bohemian only in the less generally accepted meaning of the term. Beatniks and their successors are rebels against a smug society; they consciously reject accepted values and express that rejection in a marked neglect of external appearances. Villon never rejected society; it rejected him. Throughout all his life he fervently wished to return into society's folds. He would not today understand the attitude of the hippies, even if it were articulately expressed.

A bohemian he was only inasmuch as this word refers to

the destitute artist, as it does in Murger's stories.[10] Murger's characters are bohemians because they do not have the means to be bourgeois, and perhaps one or the other begins to like this existence after he has learned to find joy in the little things that come free of charge. But this early *bohême* is the result of poverty. Only later did the word apply to an unconventional way of life deliberately chosen. A bohemian in this sense Villon never was. He did not lead a bohemian life from choice. He was not nomadic, a vagabond, from choice. He dreamed of a house and a soft bed; he did not envy Franc Gontier who finds joy in a simple life; he would like to be "a fat canon in a well-matted room" with a pretty mistress at his side and an inexhaustible supply of wine and hippocras.

The Romantic lover, too, has been eliminated. The introduction of the "Legacy" is pure invention in the most rigidly conventional style, as is the early *ballade* with the names Françoys and Marthe in acrostic. The more mature Villon of the "Testament" laughs at such pretense and urges the bearer of the message to use more appropriate terms: "Orde paillarde, d'où viens tu?" ("You filthy whore, where have you been?")

Even a disillusioned Romantic lover could not possibly address his ladylove in such a manner.

Certainly Villon was no impractical dreamer who unknowingly became involved with thieves. When he began to steal, he knew perfectly what he was doing.

A patriot he may have been, especially in the sense that he loved Paris. The "good girl from Lorraine" was much talked about during his childhood. If many of the nobles and the leading bourgeois were, on the whole, satisfied with their English allegiance, the common people were not, and the presence of an English garrison inside the walls did not help much. The old people remembered well that Joan of Arc or, in their words, "la brave Pucelle," had tried to recapture the city for the king. If she had failed, they said, it was only because her noble captains were jealous of her and did not obey her orders. At that time François was not a student yet, or else he would have heard her condemned as a heretic and a witch, the position taken by the university at that time. In the neighborhood she was well spoken of, and her death at the stake was recognized for the disgusting act of vengeance it was. People spoke of it with horror. Villon did not have to be a great patriot for this reminiscence to come up in his mind when he composed his *ballade* of the departed ladies.

The other patriotic *ballade,* in which the enemies of France are threatened with fantastic punishment may not even have been written by Villon. If it were, it would reveal little more than an almost childish pleasure in accumulated information. It is a hodge-podge of mythological, historical, and biblical references; only in the refrain does it say that all these things should happen to the enemies of France.

Thus the image of the great patriot dissolves like that of the Romantic lover. Yet in one of his fictional "biographies," Montcorbier-Villon appears as an undercover agent who thwarts one English-Burgundian intrigue after the other while persecuted by stupid authorities who mistake him for a criminal. This story, which does not have a shadow of a foundation, was very popular; it was even made into a movie in the days of the silent films.[11]

It is more difficult to explain how it came about that men like Swinburne, Rossetti, or, in a different way, Robert Louis Stevenson were so greatly attracted by Villon. These men were in a process of liberation from the shackles of Victorian propriety. For a person still laboring at breaking his chains, the sight of what seems to be an entirely free man is a great comfort. They see that it is possible after all, to be free. They envy him who has succeeded and emulate him. Hence the brother-feeling. In the case of Swinburne there also was poetic talent and a longing for a poetic form unknown in Tennysonian England. To Swinburne, Villon seemed to combine the two things he valued most: freedom of personality and easy mastery of exacting poetic form. Here was juicy substance and here was pure form.

For the juicy substance neither Swinburne nor Rossetti was ready. Their rebellion and emancipation had not gone beyond a certain point. The solid structure of their system of values could be shaken, but not torn down. They could not possibly get rid of certain notions as to what is proper and what is not. It was easier for them to squeeze their image of Villon into a slightly modified English mold rather than to adapt themselves to what he really was. They were, of course, not aware of this. They believed they had caught the essence of the man, yet they saw in him only what they were ready to see.

"Villon, our sad bad glad mad brother's name." *Sad?* Yes indeed, he was often sad. He was sad because he did not have that house and that soft bed, sad about his poverty that forced him to risk his life by stealing. *Bad* he was in the Victorian sense, but also in his own sense, when far too often he dismissed the argument of his "heart." *Glad* he must frequently have been, glad about a successful robbery or a well turned out *ballade*. He clearly reveals an uncommon capacity for intense joy.

As for the word "mad," it is completely without meaning. I should say that he was as mad as you and I and Algernon Charles Swinburne, as mad as anybody with a slight share of sensitivity.

Swinburne's *ballade* is great for its formal excellence, but there is something laborious in this rich profusion of rare rimes, this frequent accumulation of one-syllable words, as in the *refrain* or in lines such as this: "Poor kind wild eyes so dashed with light quick tears."

One never has this feeling of a successful *tour de force* with Villon himself, although, except in a few cases, his lines are just as polished, his rimes just as perfect, and, above all, melodious. In our day the traditional concepts of poetic form have been completely discarded, so completely indeed that the feeling for purely formal beauty has weakened. In the Classical period of French literature great attention, too great perhaps, was paid to purity of form. Boileau said the wrong thing about Villon, but the smoothness of Villon's form had been recognized and appreciated by a man who shared Boileau's views.

If there are formal negligences in Villon they are not neglect of meter and rime, but flaws in composition. Sometimes the given pattern or rimes caused him to fill in words or whole lines that add nothing to the meaning. In the famous *ballade* about the departed ladies is the line following the statement of what happened to Abelard: "Pour son amour ot ceste essoyne." ("for his love of her he had that misfortune.") Now this line adds nothing except the required rime in -oyne. Similarly, in the *envoi*, after asking his nostalgic question, the poet enjoins the prince not to inquire this week, nor even this year, where they are. This is very awkward and weak.

Yet there are few such flaws in the work of Villon. He is sometimes reproached for bad taste, but such pronouncements have little meaning. We no longer believe with Boileau that there could be such a thing as a good taste of permanent validity. We are more historically oriented, and so we know that the concepts of taste change even more rapidly than do the concepts of right and wrong.

"Villon sut le premier," says Boileau, and then he goes on saying the wrong thing; but thus far he is right. Villon was, indeed, the first one not "to disentangle the confused art of our old romancers" but to dare put himself into his work. To appreciate this fully one would have to survey the entire vernacular literature of Europe from the twelfth century on. It is a great and rich literature, but completely dominated by set conventions, especially in the lyrical output. In such poems as the "Sirventes," in which views rather than feelings are expressed, the personality of the individual Troubadour can be seen somewhat more distinctly. What we know about Bertran de Born or Walter von der Vogelweide we learn from their political songs.

As for the poetry of feelings, it would have been accepted only so long as it conformed with the rules. If it had deviated in the least, it would have been condemned and the poet decried as an ignorant boor. If there was one thing all the medieval poets feared, it was to appear original. To be original in lyrical poetry would have been the same thing as inventing one's own table manners.

The twelfth, the thirteenth, and the fourteenth centuries had never allowed any but the well-mannered poets to become known. To be sure, there are occasional outcries of genuine feeling. Rutebeuf, in the thirteenth century, had allowed the world to know how poor he was and how badly he had treated his poor wife.[12] But Rutebeuf was not a gentleman and did not pretend to be one. A professional minstrel could be pardoned such ill-mannered outbursts.

We have seen that Charles d'Orléans, Villon's protector at Blois, adhered all his life to the standards of the past age. His delicate, sensitive nature permeates his lovely poems, but he never allowed himself to depart from the ideal of "measure," that Aristotelian concept of virtue as the middle road between two objectionable extremes. He was, and remained, well groomed. Even when, as a prisoner in England, he sang of his longing for France, he was careful to adhere to a pattern. He did make the most of this pattern, filled it with all the permissible feelings, and did this extremely well. He was unquestionably a great poet.

Villon, we have seen, at first also attempted to fill the old pattern. The opening stanzas of the "Legacy," the "Françoys-Marthe" *ballade* and the one given to Robert d'Estouteville in no way announce the Villon of the "Testament" and of the great *ballades*.

> In the thirtieth year of my life,
> When I had drunk all my degradations ...

This is the new Villon, the one who dares make himself, his sufferings and his specific circumstances the subject of a continuous outpour. This is, indeed, an entirely novel kind of lyricism. We are so accustomed to this concept of lyrical poetry as a revelation of things experienced that we may find it difficult to see how extraordinary this was after three centuries of unchanging convention.

Villon, then, was the first to write primarily about what he had experienced personally, at least the first to do so on such a large scale.

He himself saw the good maître Jean Cotart stagger home, heard him shout, "Help, my throat is on fire!" and saw the bad bruise on his head. It was his own dear old ignorant mother for whom he wrote the prayer. It was the very real anticipation of a frightful experience that gave him the vision of himself and five others rotting and eaten by birds and swinging back and forth and around at the whim of the wind. I cannot help seeing in the disgusting and yet so marvelously plastic picture of his life with Fat Margot a true reminiscence of something experienced.

Villon would be the first to agree that it was a most shameful experience. He often disregarded the sound advice of his "heart," but he never denied that the heart was right. There is no hypocrisy in his own evaluation of himself. He will try to do what stronger men than he have done: he will stubbornly declare that it all goes back to his bad luck; but his heart knows better.

Not the slightest trace of hypocrisy is to be found in his adherence to his religion. God is the supreme ruler. He will allow Fortune to play her evil tricks on men, but only so far. Even the harsh inprisonment in Meung is something "God has permitted to happen." The bishop and his henchmen had no right to treat him so badly, and he finds it difficult to pardon them when he pardons everybody else. But let God be the judge.

The hanged men urge the onlookers to pray for them so

that God may absolve them. There is no indication anywhere that Villon was afraid of hell. His mother has this fear when she looks at the painting in the church and sees "the damned being boiled," but Villon had full confidence in the God of mercy who, after allowing certain things to happen, would ultimately straighten out the accounts.

Frivolous or even blasphemous statements prove nothing to the contrary. It is astonishing how much of this was perfectly compatible with sincere faith. The anonymous author of *Aucassin et Nicolette* has his hero protest strongly that he does not wish to go to heaven where he would have to endure the presence of all those "creeps" who hang around churches all the time; he wants to go to hell where he will have better company. In the German version of *Tristan and Isolde,* God is shown as performing a miracle to condone a false oath. Isolde has to swear that no man had ever had carnal relations with her except her husband, and to give her oath greater validity she has to undergo the ordeal of the hot iron. But since the ceremony is to take place on an island in the river, the lovers can resort to a rather crude trick. Tristan, disguised as a pilgrim, carries her to the island, and therefore she may swear that she was never in anybody's arms but in her husband's and, of course, that pilgrim's, as everybody had clearly seen. After that, she boldly picks up the hot iron, and God, who is kindly disposed toward lovers, miraculously protects her hands from being burned. This story was read and listened to with delight, and no one thought any less of God for having sanctioned perjury.

Violent and sarcastic attacks on the clergy were likewise compatible with full and sincere acceptance of the Church as a divine institution. In Dante's hell there are more popes and bishops than other people, yet no one would doubt the sincerity of Dante's faith.

Nor is there real contradiction between Villon's pity for himself and his full realization of his own depravity. The frequently repeated statement that his depravity had been caused by the ill-fortune of poverty in no way lessens the depravity itself. On the other hand, his deserved punishment does not excuse the excessive cruelty of Thibaut d'Aussigny and, later, of the provost. God had "kindly" permitted him to be punished, but He would, nonetheless, hold the perpetrators of the punishment to account.

Villon's complete works find room in one small volume. I do not believe we have reason to deplore the loss of his first work, the novel of the *Pet au Diable*. It could not have been very much, although it was naturally very popular in student circles.

In the forty well-constructed stanzas of the "Legacy" we find the first examples of Villon's indomitable humor and a few personal touches. It is in the "Testament" that the poet has first revealed himself.

Of the sixteen *ballades* included in the "Testament," we may safely discard two—those about the departed men—and we need take only slight notice of the "Françoys-Marthe" *ballade* and the one given to Robert d'Estouteville. These latter two definitely belong to the earlier period when Villon had not yet quite found himself. Twelve, therefore, remain which reveal some facet or other of our poet. Still among them are such inane items as the recipe for frying envious tongues and the humorous praise of the Parisian women. Among the remaining *ballades* are the departed ladies, the brilliant character sketch of maître Cotart, Fat Margot, the rebuttal to Franc Gontier's way of life and the prayer for his mother. Add to this the independent poems that are not *ballades*, such as the regrets of the Belle Heaulmière and the pretty *rondeau* for Ythier Marchant.

As for the "Testament" itself, it is only in part what it purports to be. A large portion of it is occupied by general remarks on many things and musings about his own strange destiny.

He had left out of his "Testament" several of his earlier

poems, such as the *ballades* on good advice, proverbs, small talk, and counter-truths, all four of which stand at the beginning of the miscellaneous poems. They are followed in that collection by the *ballade* which threatens the enemies of France, an inferior work that may not be by Villon at all. On the other hand, we may thank the unknown early editors for having included the *rondeau* which urges Jenin l'Avenu to take a bath, whether written by Villon or not.

Villon probably never intended to publish the *ballade* proposed by Charles d'Orléans. It was the kind old duke who preserved it for us. When, how, and, above all, why the insipid praise of the infant princess was preserved is unknown, and it is equally unknown at what period of his life Villon sent his humorous request for money to the Duke of Bourbon.

The remaining poems were all written after Meung, including the ironical call for help. It can only have been after his return that he wrote the important "Debate between Heart and Body," and his attempt to understand the problem of Fortune.

What is left is all connected with his last known imprisonment and the death sentence: the bold "Quatrain," the immortal "Ballade of the Hanged," the impossible poem of thanks to the Parlement, and the grimly humorous "Ballade to Garnier" referring to his appeal.

Add the seven incomprehensible *ballades* in jargon, and that is all. It is not much, but a little part of it is enough to place Villon among the great poets.

Swinburne and Stevenson tried very hard to separate the poet from the man. In the second line of the *envoi* of his own *ballade*, Swinburne says, "A harlot was thy nurse, a God thy sire."

We who are no longer Victorians are not so terribly baffled by the apparent contrast. We are inclined to think that the poet was so great because the man was what he was. We may join him in deploring his wretched luck. We shall agree with him when he presents himself as a victim of extreme harshness. On the whole, we are quite ready to comply with his own wish: to appreciate his poetry, to give the man our warm sympathy, and to leave it to God to judge him.

Notes and References

1. The principal English poems inspired by Villon, including the poetic translations by John Payne and Heron Lepper, are all contained in one volume published in New York, 1924, by Liveright.

2. Boileau's two lines on Villon are found in the middle of the second Canto of his "Art Poétique," wherein he begins a short résumé of French literature.

3. Jacques Coeur. The date of his birth is unknown, but it must have been around 1400. He was born in Bourges, where he later prospered as a merchant whose international connections became more and more extended. Among other things, he succeeded in establishing profitable affiliations with the important trading houses of Alexandria and thus could obtain silk and spices at a much lower cost than his competitors. He became proverbially rich and built a palace which is now the chief tourist attraction in Bourges. He outsmarted many of the Italian traders who were likewise amassing great wealth. But unlike those Italians who became the leading men in their city-states Coeur had to cope with the concentrated royal power of France. At the head of the royal treasury from 1440 to 1451, he enabled the king to provide his armies with the best artillery. Yet the king wanted more, and so Jacques Coeur was accused of misappropriation of funds, was imprisoned and sentenced to lose his entire fortune. He succeeded in escaping to Greece, where he hoped to build up his fortune again, but he died in 1456, still a poor man, on the island of Chios. Seven years later, the new king, Louis XI, had Coeur's sentence revised. He was declared innocent, and a small fraction of his fortune was restored to his heirs.

4. Gaston Paris, 1839-1903, was one of the most important French philologists. He edited many medieval texts. He com-

bined meticulous study of the Old French language with a keen critical sense and deep comprehension of literary values.

5. Till Eulenspiegel (variously spelled according to different German and Flemish dialects; the name means "Owl's buttocks") is the prototype of the successful prankster and master of trickery. Literally hundreds of stories were told about him in the fourteenth, fifteenth, and sixteenth centuries. Some few of these stories were collected in manuscripts and later in printed books. If Till was mainly known in the Low German country, his eastern counterpart, the Turk Nasreddin Hodja (also Khodja), is still today the hero of innumerable tales all over the Balkan countries.

6. Auguste Longnon was the scholar who established an authoritative text of Villon's poems by a careful comparison of all manuscripts and early printed versions. He also discovered many legal documents referring to Villon and found evidence that Villon and Montcorbier may have been the same person.

7. Swinburne's *Ballade* is reprinted in the same volume (New York: Liveright, 1924) that also contains his translations of individual poems along with the complete translations of Payne and Lepper.

8. This essay, which is simply entitled "Villon," is one of the last critical works of the great scholar.

9. Clément Marot, 1496-1544, was the son of a court poet and himself a poet. Active at the court of Francis I since 1522, he undertook to sort and revise the printed versions of Villon's poems. He published his own edition in 1533.

10. Henri Murger, 1822-1861, a French writer of German origin, was fascinated with the wits and lightmindedness of destitute artists and would-be artists. He popularized the word *bohême* as a term for that way of life. His "Scènes de la Vie de Bohême" were also the source of Puccini's rather sentimental opera *La Bohême*.

11. This film version, in which William Farnum played the role of Villon, was based on a musical comedy by Rudolf Friml, *The Vagabond King*, which was, in turn, based on a play by J. H. McCarthy, first performed in 1901. The title of this play, strangely enough, was *If I Were King*.

12. Rutebeuf was a thirteenth-century minstrel of great skill.

The word "minstrel" at that time denoted a professional composer of verse who may or may not have been able to write, but who produced poems for others. Rutebeuf's specialty was satires. In these he frequently expressed his own views rather than those of the persons who had commissioned him. He was also the author of a very stirring play on the clerk Theophilus, that forerunner of Faust who had sold his soul to the devil but was saved from hell by the intercession of the Virgin Mary.

Selected Bibliography

PRIMARY SOURCES

Villon, François, *Oeuvres Complètes*, publiées avec une étude sur Villon, des notes etc. par Louis Moland, Paris, Garnier.

Villon, Françoys, *Les Oeuvres*. Texte établi par A. Longnon, revu et publié par L. Foulet. Paris, Rombaldi, 1935.

Villon, Françoys, *The Complete Works*. Translated by Anthony Bonner, New York, Bantam Books, 1960.

SECONDARY SOURCES

Lepper, Heron, *The Testaments of François Villon*, New York, Liveright, 1924.

Payne, John, *Introduction* to his translation, reprinted and provided with additional notes by H. Lepper, in the above volume.

Swinburne, Algernon, *The Ballad of François Villon*, likewise reprinted, along with a few of his *Translations*, in the above volume.

Paris, Gaston, *Villon*, Paris, Hachette, 1901.

Stevenson, Robert Louis, *Essay on Villon*. In "Familiar Studies of Men and Books," New York, Scribner's, 1905.

Champion, P., *François Villon, sa vie et son temps*, Paris, 1913.

Wyndham Lewis, D. B., *François Villon, a Documented Survey*, New York, 1928.

Journal d'un Bourgeois de Paris, 1405-1449. ed. by Tuétey, 1881.

Pirenne, H., *Les Villes du Moyen-Age*, Brussels, 1924.

Rörig, F., *Die europäische Stadt*, Breslau, 1921.

Strieder, J., *Die Genesis des modernen Kapitalismus*. Leipzig, 1904.

Strieder, J., *Jakob Fugger der Reiche. Leipzig,* 1924.

Huizinga, J., *Der Herbst des Mittelalters.* München, 1928.

Curtius, E. R., *Europäische Literatur and lateinisches Mittelalter.* Bern, 1948.

Von Boehn, M., *Moden und Menschen im Mittelalter.* München, 1925.

Index